Forked

How the Greedy, the Over-Religious, and the Dumb Make Life Miserable for the Rest of Us— And What to Do about It

by Neal Starkman

Contents

Introduction

We live in a society that's increasingly affected by three groups of people—those besotted by, respectively, money, religion, and dumbosity. Any societal ill—from polluted waterways to an inadequate infrastructure to abrogation of your civil rights to your inability to land a well-paying job—is exacerbated by the impact of these people. Put another way, the level of our misery is directly correlated to their numbers and power. Think of a three-tined fork, with each tine piercing the body of our national politic.

We are getting forked.

This book will delineate just how these people control our lives—how they squelch progress, how they perpetuate injustice, and, perhaps most frustratingly, how they tend to discourage those of us who want to effect positive change. In this book, I will attempt to illustrate the motivations and the social and political dynamics behind their actions. For before we can defeat this tripartite menace, we must understand it for what it is—with only slight exaggeration, an evil that threatens to destroy us all.

In Chapter 1, "Where We're Headed," I extrapolate the behaviors from the past decade or so to give you a glimpse of our possible future—the apocalypse that awaits us should the forces of the Fork completely take over. In Chapters 2, 3, and 4, I inspect more closely the constituencies that comprise these three groups: "The Greedy," "The Over-Religious," and "The Dumb." In Chapter 5, "The Media," I show how accessibility is not always the friend it appears—how lies and calumny disseminate throughout the ether and find receptive ears and brains. In Chapter 6, "Schools," I delve into the pedagogies that foster such passive thinking and put forward some that might foster critical thinking. In Chapter 7, "Exemplars," I profile individuals and organizations that may yet lead us out of the morass and into a land of truth, justice, and what many consider, ideally, the American way. In Chapter 8, "A Better Situation," I offer an alternative to the Fork, a way that lets the greedy, the over-religious, and the dumb live in peace but not in a way that causes the rest of us—and themselves—harm. In Chapter 9, "The Thing in the Sky," I facilitate a discussion about a scenario in which the fate of our world depends in part on the attitudes and behaviors of people representing the tines of the Fork. And in Chapter 10, "What to Do," I offer some possible directions we might take to prevent doom.

This is not intended to be a book of supercilious putdowns; it's a book of awareness. Its goal is to make readers more conscious of what threatens them every day and to suggest ways to minimize those threats.

Throughout this book, I cite numerous individuals, articles, and studies to bolster my points. Invariably, as my footnotes attest, these citations are false: No such individuals, articles, and studies exist; or if they do, it's a stark coincidence, because I haven't looked them up. I take this approach for two reasons. The first reason is that I want to illustrate the way most of us currently take in information: We rarely check sources; we rarely question authority; we rarely look beyond the platitudinous headlines of a quotation, a profile, or a finding. And so I'll count on you readers to provide the validation for what you believe and the repudiation of what you don't. The second reason is that it's a lot easier to write without the needless toil of research and corroboration, and it's so much more fun.

One final note: To those of you who feel that I've written this in an idealistic hope to make the world better, you're absolutely right. To those of you who feel that I've used irony and sarcasm to highlight something that particularly vexes me, you're absolutely right.

Chapter 1
Where We're Headed

A mid-level executive in a North Carolina import company didn't want his name to be used, but he said this in a lengthy interview over the course of a Sunday and Monday:

> Look, we'd be nuts not to push for legislation that favors us; that's what this is all about. And we'd be nuts not to try to put down legislation that goes against us. All this bullshit about, well, we have to do what's right for everyone—that's what it is, bullshit. This is a tough world; capitalism is tough. And if I care about my family and my company, I'm going to do what I'm told to do. Sometimes that isn't very pretty, but there it is.[1]

Meanwhile, Reverend John Dykstra[2] is head of the Assembly of God in Coldwater, Michigan. He makes no excuses for his church's behavior:

> We do God's will. I am lucky enough to receive communications from God and articulate enough to pass those communications on to my church brothers. I would be sinning if I ignored or somehow countermanded what God wants. If people are hurt by what we do, then it must be what God has in mind. I don't question; I follow.

And this is from Eve Wellington[3], a second-grade teacher in Albuquerque, New Mexico, when I asked her about whether she thought President Barack Obama was a Muslim:

> Well, I guess he is. He's never denied it, and there's plenty of proof that he was in one of those, um, Muslim schools in Asia, or Africa, where he grew up. Listen, if he had his way, we would be living under, what is it, Sharia law before my kids get old enough to vote. And then it would be too late. Hey, I believe in America, and everything I've seen says that he—Obama—doesn't. He hates America.

You'll hear more from these people in later chapters. They—the profiteer, the devout religionist, and the terrifyingly clueless—represent great numbers of U.S. citizens. And much data indicate that their numbers are increasing. They influence others, they vote, and in certain circumscribed instances, they can affect the content of legislation. To this point—and I'm writing in 2015—they've succeeded in making the gap between rich and poor increasingly wider, in persecuting vast numbers of U.S. citizens because of some perceived religious transgression, in sending soldiers off to kill and die in unnecessary combat, and in doing immeasurable damage to the environment, foreign relations, civil rights, and education. They've also installed like-minded individuals in all levels of legislative, judicial, and executive power.

It will only get worse.

It will get worse in both subtle and gross ways. Here's a look at the subtle: Justice Richard A. Descant[4] sits on the U.S. District Court with sway over a good part of the southwest United States. He's had his share of interesting cases, and this is his overriding philosophy, as stated in an interview with the San Diego *Ledger*[5]:

> I am quite familiar with the rule of law. I am also quite familiar with both the Old and New Testaments of the Bible. I use the former to provide rationale for my decisions, and I use the latter to inform my decisions in the first place. I don't use religion as a basis to rule from the Court; I use it as the primary spur to my thinking. The difference between me and a preacher is basically this: The preacher interprets the Word of God and communicates that to his flock. I interpret the Word of God and enshrine it in case law.

Justice Descant and others like him who sit on judicial benches throughout the country may or may not make headlines because they ruled, say, against a homosexual fired from his job because he was a homosexual. But in hundreds of cases *not* in the headlines, they will have an effect on precedence— the building up of judicial decisions against homosexuals, against women, against Muslims, against atheists, against anyone who runs afoul of what someone was reputed to have said over two thousand years ago. These judges are amassing a pillar of ignorance and intolerance—enshrined, as Descant ingenuously puts it, in case law.

And the gross? How will things get worse in gross ways?

Nationally, every two years we elect members of the Fork—soulless industrialists, religious fanatics, morons. But the numbers are increasing. When we reach a point when the Fork has a majority in Congress, you can expect any of the following:

- limits on the speech and other behaviors of people who make less than a certain income

- the removal of all restrictions on any weapons for personal use

- the elimination of many federal programs, including Social Security, Medicare, student loans, workplace safety, environmental health, and unemployment compensation

- the nuclear bombing of a sovereign country that is behaving in a "non-Christian" way

- the disenfranchisement of homosexuals, Muslims, atheists, and anyone else who doesn't sign a Christian political creed as a prerequisite to voting

Farfetched? Look at the history. Look at the record. Look at what current members of the U.S. House and Senate have already advocated in the way of policies regarding money, guns, federal programs, Muslim countries, and the rights of non-Christians.

And the populace is typically taken in by banalities, deception, and outright lies. Consider the results from a variety of surveys administered in the past decade[6]:

- 81% agree with the statement, "People who have earned a high income should be able to use their wealth to lawfully access governmental services, even if those services are not readily accessible to others."

- 85% agree with the statement, "The U.S. Constitution gives American citizens the right to own weapons and to use them lawfully."

- 52% agree with the statement, "There is nothing in the U.S. Constitution that guarantees the existence of a Department of Education."

- 69% agree with the statement, "Because the United States was founded as a Christian country, there is no reason to keep Christian thought outside government policies."

- 62% agree with the statement, "Countries who display a total disregard for Christian values should not expect the United States to look favorably upon them."

- 58% agree with the statement, "Voting is a privilege, and it's not asking too much for American citizens to subscribe to the values that have made this country great in order to exercise that privilege."

Of course, the items on these surveys were worded in such a way to maximize positive responses and to provide impetus for certain causes, and the surveys themselves were sponsored by "interested parties." Conveniently left out were facts integral to an understanding of the pertinent issues, e.g., governmental services should be readily accessible to all, the Constitution doesn't give Americans *carte blanche* to use weapons, there is nothing in the U.S. Constitution that denies the existence of a Department of Education, the United States wasn't founded as a Christian country, many issues determine whether the United States "looks favorably upon" a country, and voting is a right. Nonetheless, thousands of U.S. citizens either ignored the bias of the survey item or found something sympathetic with the statement.

Professor of Sociology Emmett Barnes[7] of Silmonac University puts it this way:

> Beneath civilized exteriors often lurk less than collegial interpersonal dynamics. People aren't always as forgiving, as generous, as tolerant, as *loving* (his italics) as they make themselves out to be. It's not as simple as "People are evil"; it's more that "People are selfish in order to protect themselves." For thousands of years, we've learned that two-facedness is key to survival: We put on a good show so that we're accepted in the group, but when the opportunity arises, we're out

for ourselves and our families. This isn't good or bad; it just is.

Think of it like this: The "less than collegial interpersonal dynamics" lurking beneath our civilized exteriors cited by Dr. Barnes need only someone to puncture those exteriors, to lift the lid and expose our selfish and lazy selves. And these days, that someone is Rush Limbaugh or Sarah Palin or Ted Cruz or Mitch McConnell or any number of influence-wielders who are only too happy to roil the citizenry in the furtherance of their own ends, whether those ends are power, fame, money, or even mere popularity.

As I'll show in later chapters, this tendency is spurred by two institutions that, it could be argued, are failing us—media and schools. The former give millions of people access to the words and gestures of millions of other people, guaranteeing large numbers of acolytes, no matter what the political stance. The latter, through their dereliction of teaching critical thinking, assure that equally large numbers of people will succumb to the slightest rhetorical machinations and sign up for ever more dastardly movements.

To be sure, it's a sorry state of affairs, and it will become sorrier, especially for smart non-rich non-Christians. What has characterized the U.S. economy over at least the past several years? For one thing, the tax rate on the very rich has diminished considerably, and that's not even counting the enormous number of loopholes that multimillionaires and corporations can use to avoid paying any taxes at all. For another, members of the Republican Party and their Tea Party allies have based much of their proposed policies on the need to cut expenditures. And their way to cut expenditures is to attack public services they disagree with, such as National Public Radio and Planned Parenthood. On the state level, numerous Republican legislatures have used the need to cut expenditures as a way to attack organized labor, such as by banning collective bargaining.

What fuels these economic trends? Simply put, the very rich pay off legislators. I'm a U.S. Congressman. In order to have won my seat, I had to spend lots of money. People promised to give me money if I'd espouse certain policies that favored them, say, tax cuts or removal of environmental regulations. Maybe I already believed in these policies; if so, I could more ethically behave the way I do, and maybe it would sound less like bribery. Nonetheless, the people who support these policies have much more money than the people who support higher taxes or more environmental regulations, so it's a happy marriage. That's one tine of the Fork—the corporatists.

But I'm also careful to relate the economic situation to certain social policies. The religious right can organize a voting bloc efficiently because it's based on authority: You do what your priest/minister (on behalf of your God) tells you to do. If abortion is a sin and Planned Parenthood provides abortion services, then you vote for the person who will try to get rid of Planned Parenthood. If homosexuality is a sin and national public radio features homosexuals in a positive light, then you vote for the person who will try to get rid of the Public Broadcasting System. And if your priest/minister (on behalf of your God) tells you that Jesus believed in the free market and that any constraints at all on that free market constitute a sin, then you vote for the person who will give corporations as much latitude as possible. That's the second tine of the Fork—the religionists.

The third tine transcends the other two. That's because a large portion of the American electorate can be persuaded to vote for just about anything or anyone, given the appropriate message. These people prefer messages that are simple and clear, no matter how farfetched, no matter how unsupported by facts, even no matter how detrimental to themselves. So now we have corporations and multimillionaires spending gobs of money to disseminate such messages. The Fork has succeeded. They elect me. And I vote to do exactly what benefits my benefactors.

This does not even take into account the number of total morons who are sometimes elected to office— to mayor, to state representative, to governor, to federal representative. I am going to restrain myself from citing quotations of these people; it's too depressing. But it's not those elected officials that's the depressing part; it's the thousands of people who purposefully voted for them.

Is it any wonder that our economy is frequently in such bad shape? Sure, economists and administrators can make honest mistakes, and to some extent the economy and the behavior of individuals is unpredictable. But the Fork makes it much more difficult to anticipate problems and to react to them effectively.

A former U.S. Congressman from Delaware, John Tobin[8], speaks of the pressure he felt when confronted with voting on certain legislation:

> You may think it's easy being ethical, but you'd be wrong. I have a responsibility to do what I said I'd do during my election campaign. But no matter what I do, I'm going to disappoint somebody—some individuals, some organizations. Why should I disappoint the people who put me here as opposed to the people who voted against me? That makes no sense at all. Maybe on some occasions I'm sympathetic to the other side, but when people I know personally trust in me, it's very tough. It's not a matter of walking away from potential financial support; it's disappointing them. They had faith in me, and I'm letting them down. That's tough, let me tell you, it's really tough. It's easy to say, well, you should vote your conscience, but legislation isn't like that. There's usually something good you can find in a bill and there's usually something bad in it, so the rationalizations are inherent to the process. I did my best to do what I thought my constituents would want me to do, but the people who always supported me would get top priority; that's only natural.

Tobin was reelected seven times.

Why will things get worse? For one thing, thanks to U.S. Supreme Court rulings, rich people have many more opportunities to reach U.S. citizens with their messages: the airwaves, the Internet, and at least one entire television and radio network (Do you know what scat sex is? Look it up; I had to. Fox News is to news as scat sex is to sex). For another thing, issues are becoming more complex, and information is becoming abundant, so people are discouraged from checking the veracity of such information on their own and opt for simple explanations and solutions. And for another, the worse the economy gets, the more people cling to "isms" to help them out—doctrines that sound good but that may be erroneous or harmful or both.

This last point bears emphasis, and I'll use an old Georgian (that's the country, not the state) tale[9] to illustrate it:

> A farmer was beset with problems. His crop had failed for the second year in a row, his wife was pregnant again, his older son refused to work, and his younger son had developed a severe cough that no one wanted to admit was getting worse. Amidst these troubles, the farmer's brother visited from the other side of the county and sold him a "miracle" fertilizer that promised to "turn your crop fertile within a fortnight." The farmer applied the fertilizer and waited the allotted time. When nothing happened, he went to his wife and said, "The fertilizer didn't work; I probably did something wrong." "How could you do

anything wrong?" she asked. "It's fertilizer. You sow it into the ground and you water it." "Never mind that," responded the farmer. "I'll get some more and make it work. It has to work, because it's worked before." "You trust this fertilizer more than you trust yourself?" asked his wife. The farmer nodded. "I trust myself to worry about our sons and our yet-to-be-born. I trust fertilizer to grow our crops."

There are a lot of Georgian farmers out there. They are so beset with problems that when something comes along promising a "fertile crop"—a self-improvement book, a religion, an economic policy, a diet, a candidate—they buy it. They're buying hope, and trust. They're buying solace from having to think and worry about yet another trouble in their lives. They don't want to examine this new fertilizer, or to question its provenance, or to doubt its claims. They want it to work. And if perchance it doesn't work, then they blame themselves or someone else, but they remain open to purchasing new fertilizers.

The problem, of course, is that many fertilizers are literally pure crap. They don't work, they've never worked, and they're sold by hucksters to naifs or to people who desperately want to believe in them. But the worse things get in this country, the more people will want to find some part of their lives that can be easily calmed. They don't want to think about it, they don't want to work for it, they just want their problems solved. And they'll buy the fertilizer. People turn to religion in hard times. The poorest nations on earth are the most religious. And the poorest people are generally the most religious. They tell themselves that the fertilizer works.

So, where are we headed? When things get worse, some people want to sell more fertilizer and others want to buy it. The spiral becomes a maelstrom, sucking everyone—even, eventually, the sellers—down into it. We can stop this spiral, but it requires work. And sometimes people aren't willing to work until they see no alternative.

Before we delve into potential solutions, though, I want to more closely analyze the three tines of the Fork. We'll start with ostensibly the most powerful tine: the corporations and their representatives who have taken advantage of our economic system to make the division between rich and poor in this country greater than it has ever been.

Chapter 2
The Greedy

This is Llewellyn C. Carson[1], the CEO of National Digital, speaking at his company's annual conference, Syracuse, New York, 2010:

> It's time we stopped apologizing for being successful. I say to you, I am proud that this company is profitable. I am proud that this company is making money. And yes, I am proud that this company takes advantage of every single tax loophole and government benefit that is available to us. Ladies and gentlemen, making a profit while providing a product or service is what made this country great. This is capitalism. And we'd be fools to ignore any legal means to maximize that profit. You'd get rid of me before the next rise of the sun, and I'd deserve it. So the next time you hear someone lambaste a company like this one for "making too much of a profit" or "taking advantage of loopholes," tell that person we're following the law, we're doing what we're supposed to do, and we're contributing to the great system that is America. No apologies, goddammit! No apologies!

He's got a point—to a point. It's certainly true that the American capitalist system encourages companies to make large—to some people, obscene—profits. If, as Carson maintains, a company legally takes advantage of everything possible to make money, it's not technically at fault. However, as Kent says in "King Lear," "That is not the whole of the tale."[2]

If you're rushing down the street trying to make an appointment, and someone stumbles in front of you and falls down, you have a choice: You can stoop to help the person up, thereby spending an extra, say, 15 seconds more than you'd planned; or you can ignore the person and be sure to make your appointment on time. There's no law that says you have to stop and help, but most people would agree that it would be the right thing to do.

If you win a pie in a contest, you have a choice: You can eat the whole thing yourself, keeping it in the refrigerator for a week or as long as it takes to finish it; or you can offer to share it with a friend or family member. In this case, not only would most people agree that sharing it would be the right thing to do, but it would probably also give you some pleasure to do so.

If your company makes tons of money, you have a choice: You can keep the profits for yourself, your co-administrators, and stockholders; or you can give bonuses to your staff, donate to charities, set up an educational endowment, authorize rebates to customers . . . you get the idea. In this case, my guess is that people would be more divided on what would be the right thing to do.

Does it come down to opinion, to values, even, in some cases, to religious belief? Is the meaning of life to maximize our own pleasure, to maximize others' pleasure, or to somehow find the appropriate percentages of egocentrism and altruism? (A potentially complicating factor is that many people derive pleasure from pleasing others.)

I don't know the appropriate percentages of taking care of yourself and taking care of others, but I don't believe that they're 100% and 0%, or even close to that. However, we have corporations and individuals in today's society who act as if they believe it.

The philosophy goes something like this:

"Either by hard work or cleverness or accident of birth, I've got money. With that money, I buy things to make me and the people I care about happy. It's up to me to keep as much of that money as possible, which also means that it's up to me to pay as little taxes as possible. When I pay taxes, I'm giving my money to people who haven't been as hardworking, clever, or lucky as me, and that isn't right. So I'm going to do everything I can to keep as much of my money as I can."

The "taxes" part is interesting. You've heard the counter-arguments plenty of times: "You didn't get rich without the government's help, whether it's by using government-maintained roads or receiving government-sanctioned subsidies or attending government-supported schools or even drinking water, eating food, and breathing air that's safeguarded (to some extent) by the government. So the idea that you don't owe the government anything is absurd."

But it is kind of galling, isn't it, to know that your tax dollars are going to people and to causes you disagree with? Yes, some people take advantage of government welfare. Yes, some people sponge off others rather than look for a job. That isn't news. But recognize that yes, sometimes we go and bomb the hell out of countries we shouldn't. And yes, sometimes we pay farmers to destroy crops. And yes, we probably pay members of Congress more than we should, given their extended holidays.

That's kind of what you have to do when you live in a republic.

But don't take my word for it. Here's Professor of Political Science Aaron Schwartzer[3] of the Lincoln School of Political and Economic Studies:

> Our system works best when people feel that they have been wronged. It's the tension that produces the best results. So it's fine, under certain conditions, if people complain. Having said that, though, the system doesn't work at all if the people at the economic top of the ladder don't funnel some of their money down to those on lower rungs. It's not "beneficence"; it's a guarantee that the system survives. And that's not my opinion; that's a fact.

Others clearly disagree with Dr. Schwartzer's analysis. They don't want to pay their employees more than minimum wage—if that. They don't want to pay the same percentage of taxes that their employees do. They don't want to pay for worker safety and environmental protections and medical leave and child care and human resources and anything else that compromises their bottom line. As they see it, they became rich by bringing in money, not giving it away. Maybe they made money by providing a product or service that people are willing to buy, but that's only part of the story; the other part—and sometimes it's the bigger part—is how they keep that money and make it grow.

In her book, *The Corporate Mind*, Danielle Shavey[4] makes a useful distinction between corporate behavior before "making it big" and corporate behavior afterward. The distinction is in the category but not the results: If corporate executives were heartless along their journey to become rich, they remain heartless after success. In fact, says Shavey, their behaviors are often even more ruthless once they're on the top:

> Skinner would call it "reinforcement." These people were rewarded for their treachery, their dishonesty, and their utter disregard for others. There's no reason for them to change their *modus operandi*. Why should they mess with success? Why should they suddenly do something different from what has proven to be so effective? On the contrary, now that they're confident and have more resources, their previous behaviors are only intensified. Where they might have bought up a small

mom-and-pop store and converted it into a parking lot some years ago, now they might buy up a company with a thousand employees, fire them all, and mutate it into a warehouse. The goal is the same, and the end is always justifiable.

That end—to make money and to keep it—is, as CEO Carson would say, "the American way." And really, when you look at polls and you interview people on the street or in the wheat fields, you find an astounding adherence to this philosophy. Several years ago, a polling organization out of Massachusetts—liberal Massachusetts—asked several hundred former employees of a small company that was bought up and extinguished whether they felt that the head of the extinguishing company had the right to do what he did. Fully 59 percent said, "yes"—this despite the fact that they were now out on the street as the result of that "right."[5]

However, what's even more curious is the next question and its response. The pollsters asked whether the head of the company "should have" done what he did. After all, we can agree that a person has the right to do something without that something being "right." The result? Fifty-two percent said, "yes." Post-polling interviews indicated that many respondents believed they would have done the same thing were they in those circumstances. One might argue that it's commendable for so many people to maintain an unbiased attitude toward a philosophy that hurts them. One might also argue that it's sad for so many people to put a philosophy before the well-being of themselves, their families, and their colleagues.

But let's move beyond the clear fact that people with money often make more money by "inconveniencing" others. These days, it's much, much bigger than that. And there are two basic ways in which it's bigger: politicians and issues.

Let's face it; politicians have always been bought. In the last chapter, I told you about the North Carolina import company executive who made no apologies for using money to sway legislation. And from the other side, I quoted Delaware Congressman John Tobin, who often felt compelled to enact legislation pushed by his donors. But we shouldn't forget how politicians such as Tobin get elected in the first place.

You can buy an election. Let me be clear about this: You can buy an election. That doesn't mean that the candidates with the most money behind them always win, but it sure increases the odds.

How much does it increase the odds? In the last 20 years, counting only state and federal elections, the candidates with the higher financial backing won their elections 83% of the time.[6] That's impressive. And, in elections as in many other areas, the success of the greedy—one tine of the Fork—depends on the zealotry of the over-religious and the naiveté of the dumb—the other two tines of the Fork.

It works like this: I have a lot of money, and I want Joe Suckup to be elected, or reelected. The first thing I do is get assurance from Suckup that, for the most part, he'll obey me once he's in (I can get that assurance in numerous ways, many of them legal). Next, I infuse his campaign and both his current and future advisory circle with people who think the way I do. Then, there's the money. We buy television commercials and radio commercials and social media campaigns. We finance Suckup's trips and speaking engagements around his district, whether that's a city, a state, or the country. We conduct research on Suckup's opponent(s) so we can show how bad they are. And both before and during the campaign, we use our influence to bring along media representatives who are favorably disposed toward Suckup.

We choose issues—guns, homosexuality, school prayer, abortion, immigration, whatever—that will lure the zealots in, and we frame everything in clichéd, black-and-white terms to convince the dumb—excuse me, the "low information voters"—that we're acting in their best interests.

And that's the second basic way in which people with money often make more money: They co-opt the issues.

No doubt, some rich people earnestly believe that it's every American's Constitution-given—let alone God-given—right to own and wield assault rifles. They have their rationales: We need to protect ourselves from the government, in case it suddenly goes rogue. We need to protect ourselves from marauders who attack our families at home in the middle of the night or at a convenience store in the middle of the day. We need to be able to express ourselves by shooting at firing ranges or at tin cans in our backyard or at deer in state parks—whatever. Some people believe that.

But listen: A lot of rich people *make money* if people continue to buy guns. It's so simple: If I own stock in a gun company, if I own stores that sell guns, if I buy and sell ammunition at a discount, then I make more money when laws permit—encourage—people to own and wield guns. It's no different than rich people convincing people that it's good to drill for oil in the middle of the country, or to reduce taxes on other rich people, or to permit rich people to base their corporations overseas so they don't have to pay taxes at all.

Congressional hearing on banning assault rifles, April 6, 2011[7]:

"Mr. Sawicki, I want to know: Do you or do you not own shares in Remington, Inc., which sells all manner of firearms?"

"Yes, I do. The last I looked, it was not illegal or immoral to own stock in American companies."

"You're correct, sir; I didn't imply that it was. How many shares do you own, sir?"

"I'm not aware of the actual number."

"Would it be safe to assume that you own upwards of 40% of the company?"

"I'm not aware of the actual percentage."

"Mr. Sawicki, is it not true that were this legislation to be passed and the aforementioned weapons were to be banned from public consumption, you would lose millions of dollars?"

"I'm not a prognosticator, Congressman. I own shares because I believe the company is . . . fruitful."

"Yes, I'm sure you do. Can we agree, sir, that passage of this legislation would probably not benefit you financially and in fact would cause you significant financial loss?"

"It doesn't take a rocket scientist to ascertain that."

"No. No, it doesn't. And it doesn't take a rocket scientist to ascertain that, as president of Guns for All, you don't mention your financial connections to Remington; you focus on, let's see, 'the complete, unmistakable, and unshakable import of the Second Amendment.' Isn't that true, sir?"

"No comment."

That's how it works. Money buys politicians, money buys issues.

But wait a second, I hear you say (sometimes I hear voices): "All citizens have the right to use their money to influence the state of their country and the world. Would you be so quick to denounce rich people who use their money to protect endangered species or pass legislation preventing job discrimination?"

No, of course not. For one thing, they probably wouldn't benefit financially, unless, for example, they owned preserves for spiny-tailed lemurs and would rake in the cash as all such animals were deposited in those places. But for another thing, even if they did profit, who cares? Their efforts would be helping others. That's the point. Greedy people's efforts help only themselves; if anyone else gets helped, it's incidental. Think about all the issues pushed by corporate types: How many of those issues can really be said to be designed for the greater good? I'll tell you: very few.

David Sistern[8], in his 2014 book, *The Corporate Enigma: How People Buy into Executive Fantasies and Impoverish Themselves and Others*, points out the obvious:

> Less than five percent of all legislation backed or sponsored by executives of corporations worth more than 100 million dollars could be rightfully seen as benefiting more than a handful of people besides the stakeholders of those corporations.

And in a rare, off-the-cuff interview in the British magazine, *Ltd.*, hotel tycoon Lemuel Hastings[9] candidly revealed why he was opposing both safety and environmental legislation in Parliament: "I'd lose money. I didn't get where I am by being a blithering idiot."

All this affects you greatly. Corporate executives have more influence than anyone outside the president's advisers over foreign policy. Do you think we really went into Iraq to help the poor, downtrodden Iraqi people? Do you think we would have done the same to help a country that wasn't sitting on huge amounts of oil? And before you say, "What about

Vietnam?," understand that corporations make millions of dollars off *any* war. Planes and ships and uniforms and supplies and guns and bombs and personnel aren't free: The federal government pays corporations billions of dollars to acquire them. Can you recall a major corporation urging us to get *out* of Vietnam? to get *out* of Iraq or Afghanistan?

How else does it affect you? Think of smog. Think of rapidly melting glaciers. Think of companies that spew all sorts of toxic chemicals into the air and the water. Do the chairpeople of these companies not care about the environment? Who knows? What's significant is that they value profits more than environmental protections. It costs money to clean up a disaster, but sometimes it costs more money to prevent a disaster; and if the disaster is not a one-time event but a slow creep toward doom, then it's easy to put off any kind of prevention at all. You don't see many corporate executives lobbying for more environmental protections.

And why would legislators vote against raising a minimum wage, or against measures to increase workplace safety, or, for that matter, against the 40-hour work week? Do they not care about average employees? Who knows? What's significant is that their backers lose money if they enact this legislation. Higher wages, safer work conditions, and time off work mean an erosion of the bottom line. So they man the turrets and try to maintain the status quo, workers be damned.

One more point, and this is an important one: It's not only the people "at the top" who are responsible for the perpetuation of greed in this country. People at all levels of corporations lobby at all levels of government to make sure that policies affecting corporations benefit corporations. Here is more from the interview I conducted with that mid-level executive in a North Carolina import company. We talked in his office; he was very candid, and that's probably why he didn't want his identity revealed.[10]

Executive: "Look, we'd be nuts not to push for legislation that favors us; that's what this is all about. And we'd be nuts not to try to put down legislation that goes against us. All this bullshit about, well, we have to do what's right for everyone—that's what it is, bullshit. This is a tough world; capitalism is tough. And if I care about my family and my company, I'm going to do what I'm told to do. Sometimes that isn't very pretty, but there it is."

Me: "So, are there limits to what you'll do? Suppose you're asked to push for the removal of restrictions on some medicine you know hasn't been fully tested. Wouldn't it make you feel bad if people died as a result of the legislation you pushed? What if your wife or your kids took the medicine? Wouldn't you feel responsible?"

Executive: "The legislation doesn't rise or fall because of me alone. I'm a, I don't know, a cog, okay? I'm not going to take the credit for anything that happens, and I shouldn't have to take the blame, either. Legislation is a complex process. I'm only one little . . . atom in the whole organism. Or something; you get what I mean. I'm not that important. And besides, if I thought the medicine was harmful, I wouldn't let anyone in my family buy it."

Me: "So I guess that answers my question. There are no limits. Your boss tells you to do A, B, or XYZ, and you do it."

Executive: "Hey, don't be so high and mighty! Not everyone can tell their boss to go to hell and get another job by the next Monday, you know! Not everyone can be a high-flying journalist! I do what almost everyone does at work. I take orders from someone higher up, and I give orders to someone lower down. That's how things work. And I frankly don't know enough about the . . . the *content* of what I'm doing to make the decisions that someone who's getting paid a lot more than I am is making."

There you have it: "I'm only obeying orders." It's the essential philosophy of the corporation—and, as we'll see, for the over-religious as well.

So the first tine of the Fork is dangerous in two ways: First, the goals of the greedy are often opposed to the goals of the rest of us. And second, the greedy are able to exert tremendous amounts of influence on not only the decision-makers but also on the people who vote for those decision-makers. The tine is sharp. And it can be deadly.

The second tine can also be deadly; in fact, "death to others" is sometimes key to its perceived survival.

Chapter 3
The Over-Religious

Many questions are begged here:

1. Are all religious people harmful?

2. What does it mean to be over-religious?

3. How can people be persuaded to change something in which they believe so fervently?

4. Isn't it just a matter of opinion as to whose religion is right and whose is wrong?

5. Aren't religions—and religious people—responsible for doing really good things in the world?

6. Don't atheists and agnostics and other nonbelievers do things that harm people?

And here are your answers to those questions:

1. No.

2. The people I'm concerned with are those who try to foist their attitudes, beliefs, and behaviors on others. What makes them over-religious is their fanaticism with proselytizing as well as their unswerving fealty to their religious leaders in the face of cruelty, irrationality, and intolerance.

3. It's very difficult; hence, the problem.

4. It is if you accept that it's also a matter of opinion as to whether innocent people should be suppressed, shamed, imprisoned, enslaved, raped, tortured, and killed.

5. Yes. And they probably could have—and should have—done those things without their religion.

6. Yes, but much less often than religious people.

Now that we've got that out of the way, let's proceed in an effort to understand why over-religious people are so harmful to others.

It begins with not thinking. Virtually every major religion—certainly every Christian and Muslim religion—requires its adherents not to question, not to doubt, and certainly not to ridicule its supernatural aspects. So, when God does things in the Bible that are senseless, contradictory, or gratuitously cruel, you accept it, period. When a rule comes down from on high that you're not supposed to draw a picture of Mohammed—even if you haven't a clue as to what Mohammed looked like and you have no idea how anyone could be harmed by seeing your illustration— you obey it, period. It's not that you're bowing to God; it's that you're bowing to God's representatives— priests, preachers, imams, shahs, and others. No critical thinking is involved—ever.

Now this is fine within the particular religious community—well, not for everyone, of course, such as, say, women—and in general this mind-set helps make the religion more cohesive, stronger. Everyone's on board. It's like the army. If you're a private and the sergeant tells you to do 50 push-ups for no apparent reason, you still do those 50 push-ups. That's the way everything goes down in the army. And that's the way everything goes down in many religions.

Joseph Sandler[1] is a 52-year-old Catholic priest in Acadia, Ohio. By all accounts—I haven't met him—he's very congenial, very kind. His flock loves him, and his door, as they say, is always open. If you bumped into Joseph Sandler at a party or on a cruise or at a convention, you'd probably like him immediately. He's married with three sons and a daughter, and he's been the head of his church for 17 years.

But, based on his sermons and other writings over the years, here's what Joseph Sandler believes:

- People sin constantly, and if they don't confess their sins to Sandler or another priest, they will be damned to hell for eternity.

- Women are created to serve their husbands.

- Homosexuality is a sin; homosexuals can be forgiven only by becoming heterosexual or celibate.

- Nonmarital sex is a sin.

- Sex—even heterosexual marital sex—for reasons other than procreation is a sin.

- Everything in the Bible is true, literally: Adam and Eve, the flood, the resurrection of Jesus.

Everything. To repeat: Several thousand years ago, the world was created in seven days.

- Everything in the Bible, including the slaughter of children, is justified as long as God commanded it.

- Everything that happens on earth—starvation, the Holocaust, the outcomes of football games, a person running into an old friend, a car running into an old friend, airplanes crashing into orphanages, Nicolas Cage's choice of movies—happens for a reason, known only to God.

- People who don't subscribe to Catholicism— people of other religions, mentally ill people, developmentally disabled people, children—will be damned to hell for eternity.

- You can live the most heinous of lives—killing and torturing people, stealing from people, lying to people—but if you confess your sins and pledge your fealty to God, you'll still go to heaven.

- God speaks to Joseph Sandler.

Now, the important thing to take away from this is not, wow, what a lunatic. The important thing to take away from this is that Joseph Sandler is representative of plenty of over-religious people, and not only Catholics; in many groups, he and his beliefs are the norm.

Earlier, I quoted the Reverend John Dykstra[2], head of the Assembly of God in Coldwater, Michigan. Sitting in his plush church office, he was interviewed by a very skeptical reporter from a local TV station; the interview caused great outcry when it subsequently aired. Here is more of it:

Dykstra: "We do God's will. I am lucky enough to receive communications from God and articulate enough to pass those communications on to my church brothers. I would be sinning if I ignored or somehow countermanded what God wants. If people are hurt by what we do, then it must be what God has in mind. I don't question; I follow."

Reporter: "I'm interested in how you know that the . . . communications you're receiving are from God."

Dykstra: "It's just something I know. How do you know that I'm talking to you right now?"

Reporter: "Well, I can see you, I can hear you—"

Dykstra: "And there's your answer. I can see God, I can hear God. Sometimes I think I can almost feel Him *(capitalization assumed)*. It's always a little different, but I know it's Him. And He hasn't steered me wrong yet."

Reporter: "What would be an example of 'steering you wrong'?"

Dykstra: "I can't give you an example, 'cause it's never gonna happen. Look, either you believe that God is all-present, all-knowing, and all-powerful, or

41

you don't. If you don't, then none of this is going to make any sense."

Reporter: "Okay, fair enough. But what if you heard God say, 'I want you to tell the men in your congregation to beat their wives.'—you know, to keep them in line. Would you do that? Or would you wonder, well, maybe he said '*treat* their wives.' Or maybe he said 'beat their wives,' but he meant beat them in cards or Monopoly or something."

Dykstra: *(chuckling patronizingly)* "You just don't get it, do you. I don't question what God says. That's a nonstop train to hell, if you ask me. It's not a matter of everyday hearing. I don't hear God like I hear you asking me these somewhat naïve—if you don't mind my saying—questions right now. I *know* what God tells me to do, and my congregants know that what I tell them comes directly from God, through me. That's my job. I'm a funnel through which God's desires pass. Yes, if He said 'Beat your wives,' then I'd hope and expect that every man in my congregation would go home and beat his wife. You take the bad with the good, but with God, in the long run, it's all good. And I don't question the Almighty's motives. Neither should you."

And lest you think that such religious leaders' influence stops at the doors of the church, read this testimony from Carrie Lipton[3], who with much difficulty escaped from a Mormon community several years ago; luckily, she had no children and so got away more easily than parents have been able to. What was the mind-set of members of the community?

It was unreal. It was, like, whatever the Elders said, that's what you'd do. I mean, weird. Give them your money. Slap your wife. Tell your kids this or that. It didn't matter how private it was, it was, like, well, you don't have any say in the matter, and you shouldn't have any say in the matter.

I think—I think some people, like my husband, some people liked not having to think about stuff. "Is this right or wrong?" Ask the Elder. "Should I do this or that?" Ask the Elder. It made life so much easier—well, it did, anyway, if you were on top. If you were like me, well, I'm a woman, and so, generally, if there was a dispute or any kind of question at all about something, I got the short end of the stick. It was just, like I say, weird.

It took me awhile to get readjusted after I left. I mean, it took me awhile to get readjusted when I first got there. At first, I thought, well, this is okay. It's strict, but everyone seems happy. What a pleasant place. And I was in love with my husband, and he was really into it, so, you know, why not. But slowly I came to realize, I couldn't do it anymore. I just couldn't. I, like, had a brain, and it was sort of disappearing or something.

So, like I said, it took me awhile to get back to reality after I left. But not that long. Maybe three months. And it was so nice to get away. I mean, life isn't as, you know, pleasant as it was in the community. But it, I don't know, feels more real, you know?

This tine on the Fork consists of two parts, and both parts harm us. The first part of the tine is what Ms. Lipton refers to when she says that "some people liked not having to think about stuff." People who let others do their thinking for them are often dangerous. Naturally, it depends on what the Elder, the priest, the imam, or some other authority figure says. But regardless of the message, if people rely on an authority figure rather than on facts, logic, or an objective moral code, they can persuade themselves to sanction the most outrageous acts. Did I mention the Holocaust?

The second part of the tine that harms us is the proselytizing factor. It'd be one thing if all the lunatics who didn't believe in evolution or who thought homosexuality was a sin or who viewed females as innately subservient to males kept to themselves. You want to believe in ghosts? Fine. As Jews say, *Gey gezunterheyt*, Go in good health. But don't try to make me believe in them, don't abuse me for not believing in them, don't treat me as inferior for not believing in them, and don't pass laws that give you advantages over me.

These two parts of the tine—the non-thinking and the proselytizing—combine to wreak havoc in elections. The proselytizers put forth their ideas, which are, essentially, to make everyone believe and act the way they do. And the non-thinkers follow along—not only to the proselytizers but also to whatever their "leaders" advise them.

Think about it: If you're the head guy—and it's almost always a guy—in your religion, then you can literally get your followers to do *anything*. It helps if you back it up with even higher authority, of course— a holy book, a holy person from a previous century, or the Man Himself—but for the most part, if you're charismatic and forceful and possess a patina of common sense, why, you're holding all the cards in the deck.

And lest we forget, if you're the head guy, and you're predisposed toward certain attitudes—anti-woman, anti-gay, anti-abortion, anti-other- (or -no-) religions—you can most likely find quick support in the passages of your holy book. It's so much easier for the head guy to launch a crusade when he already believes in the mission.

In her book, *The Sins They Command*, Polish author Nadia Grabowski[4], a former Catholic, provides a list of beliefs that religions have fostered in just the past 100 years. The list includes the following:

- People of Jewish descent should be avoided, isolated, or killed, depending on circumstances.

- People of Arabic descent should be avoided, isolated, or killed, depending on circumstances.

- People of African descent should be avoided, isolated, or killed, depending on circumstances.

- People of Asian descent should be avoided, isolated, or killed, depending on circumstances.

- People who are homosexual should be avoided, isolated, or killed, depending on circumstances.

- People with physical disabilities should be avoided, isolated, or killed, depending on circumstances.

- People with mental disabilities should be avoided, isolated, or killed, depending on circumstances.

- Scientists should not be trusted.

- Artists, musicians, and writers should not be trusted.

- College-educated people should not be trusted.

- Females should be treated as slaves.

- All our behaviors are controlled by a supernatural, omniscient, omnipotent being.

- Whatever happens, happens for a supernatural reason.

- It is blasphemous to question or challenge any of the above.

Why are religious leaders so successful? Why would people give up their freedom of thought? Why would they throw away everything they might have believed in the past to belong to a group that believed another way and that in fact might make life more uncomfortable for them?

The answer is easy.

No, really, the answer is easy. People find it easier *not* to think about stuff, *not* to have to make decisions, not to take responsibility for those decisions (or lack of decisions).

Imagine what it's like to live this way: All the hard thinking has already been done for you. The path, the right way, it's all there for you to follow, no questions asked. And that is an important condition: No questions asked. The truth is told to you, and you obey the rules. You don't have to worry about "Should I do this or that?" You don't have to fret about something you said or did. And, best of all, there's a supremely cool afterlife awaiting you, so no matter what happens in this life, well, after you die, that's when it gets really good.

And there's a bonus: Not only don't you have to concern yourself about what happens to you, but you also don't have to concern yourself about what happens to anyone else. The orphanage burned down? God (or Allah, or Whoever) must have had a good reason for it, whatever it was. They're all in heaven now, anyway, so no real loss. The tornado took away that young family who gave liberally to the poor, but the petty thief living next door was spared? I guess it was a miracle—I mean, from the petty thief's point of view. As I mentioned before, everything from the 9-11 terrorism to the outcome of the high school football game is predetermined.

This attitude is offered unapologetically by true believers. They trust in a higher power. That means they absolve themselves of all responsibility. But the catch is this: There are only two ways to know what that higher power is thinking. One way is to communicate through prayer, and of course many people do this, or think they do this. They have a personal connection, you see, with the Great One, and they can have kind of a dialog when it suits both of them. I don't want to be pejorative, but having this dialog is also known as schizophrenia.

The other way to know what the higher power is thinking is through that higher power's representatives, and here's where it gets really dangerous for the rest of us. Priests, preachers, shahs, imams, rabble-rousing media types of all kinds: These are the Great One's representatives, or so they say (Notice I didn't include rabbis. Jews don't believe that rabbis have any more communication with God than anyone else does; rabbis are teachers. And many Jews consider it a responsibility to question and be critical; I'm sure you've noticed this. Still, orthodox Jews are right up there with orthodox others when it comes to worshiping and "obeying" God).

So, if God's representative tells you in church that sex for reasons other than procreation is sinful—that even *nudity* is sinful—then, hey, it's got to be true. If you watch an on-line sermon about how women need to cover their faces at all times, and that sermonizer has a connection with the Great One, well, that's it, then; women should be veiled. For that matter, if you read the Bible, and it says that the Earth was created in a week, who are you to question that? I mean, should you trust some pointy-headed scientist from a liberal arts university or the holy ones who took down God's words nearly verbatim? Heck, I know which one *I'd* go with.

But, you might say, "I steer clear of those people. I don't go to that kind of church, and I'm not affected by their backward attitudes."

Think again.

I want you to meet Justice Richard A. Descant[5], U.S. District Court, Philadelphia, mentioned in the first chapter. I got a tip from a friend about some of the good justice's rulings and had to meet him. In turn, for some reason—undoubtedly because he didn't know me—he agreed to be interviewed in his chambers.

Me: "Justice Descant, you're known as someone who often quotes the Bible in your decisions. Do you ever find the teachings of the Bible at odds with the law you've sworn to uphold?"

Descant: "I am quite familiar with the rule of law. I am also quite familiar with both the Old and New Testaments of the Bible. I use the former to provide rationale for my decisions, and I use the latter to inform my decisions in the first place. I don't use religion as a basis to rule from the Court; I use it as the primary spur to my thinking. The difference between me and a preacher is basically this: The preacher interprets the Word of God and communicates that to his flock. I interpret the Word of God and enshrine it in case law."

Me: "But surely you can see where some might think you're prejudging a case based on what you've already read in the Bible?"

Descant: "People can think what they like, of course."

Me: "But do you grant that they may have a point—that you have certain views of, say, the roles of women and men, or the conflict of free speech vs. blasphemy, or, for that matter, the origins of the earth—and that these views may bias your decisions on a case involving such issues?"

Descant: "It's nonsense. People—even judges—have views on everything. For some, it may come from the Bible; for others, it may come from an encyclopedia, or a talk with a minister, or a sports magazine. It doesn't matter what my views are. I rule by law."

Me: "But you just told me that you use religion as a spur to your thinking. If you start out believing one thing, doesn't that affect your judgment?"

Descant: "You have to start out believing in something! We're not blank slates, you know. I know what you're getting at, but what you seem not to understand is that this country—and its laws—were based on ideas put forth in the Bible. There's no contradiction, no conflict, between the two. I'd be surprised, and troubled, if a rule of law somehow ran opposed to the teachings of the Bible."

Me: "But if it did: Suppose you had to decide between the law and something in, I don't know, Philippians. What would you do? No doubt that's come up before?"

Descant: *(smiling)* "No, it hasn't. I can honestly say that every judgment I have made in this courthouse has been consistent with both the law and the Christian creed. As I said, it would be a serious matter if they diverged. I think you've gotten the answers to your questions. Thank you; it's been a pleasure."

Indeed. Sad to say, there are Justice Descants throughout our good, supposedly secular nation. They have influence. They change lives. They rule from the second tine of the Fork.

And speaking of ruling from the second tine of the Fork, we do have second-tine people in our U.S. Senate and House of Representatives. Consider: If I'm a believer in deep religious orthodoxy, I've obviously shunned the requirement of rationality as a basis of judgment. So anything goes. I can vote for or against absolutely anything because of my religious beliefs. You're not going to affect me with your arguments, because your arguments are impotent against my "inner judgment." God beats logic every time.

Now the question becomes this: Why are the religious so conservative? For the beginning of the answer, I go physiological. This is from Dr. Peter Vasilov's[6] (coincidentally, a pointy-headed scientist from Yale University) 2012 tome, *The Brain, the Neurons, the Thoughts*:

> There is a systematic shift in neurological, synaptic activity when one is expanding one's thought processes, for example, when one is engaged in an open-ended "brainstorm" session, or when one is trying to solve a mystery of some sort. Conversely, the neurological, synaptic activity is markedly different— and markedly less—when one is not engaged in what we sometimes call "deep thought," that is, when one is calm, routinized, accepting of virtually everything at face value, and not causing oneself to question or probe.

It's a fact: Conservative people think differently than others do, when they think at all. But so what? So what if they listen to their leaders? Some of us listen to scientists, others of us listen to clerics. What makes the clerics and the other religious representatives so conservative?

It comes down to authority. If I've acquired a group of followers, and I want to keep those followers, then I can't permit them to think outside the box that I've provided for them. I can't tell them to be sexual, experience pleasure, grant equal freedoms to everyone, help those in need regardless of their religious persuasion. If I do that, then it's much more likely my followers will rely less on my authority and more on their own instincts. I can't have that, now can

I? I must go in the other direction: I must make adherence to my commands arduous yet doable.

Do you know what cognitive dissonance is? It's when you learn to favor something negative mainly because you've suffered so much that it provides a rationale for your suffering. The dissonance comes from wanting something yet experiencing pain in trying to attain it. You resolve the dissonance by increasing the value of the goal: It must be really worthwhile if you're hurting this much: "This wine must be really tasty, given that I spent $90 on it." On the other hand, "This medicine must be really effective, given how bad it tastes."

That's what over-religious leaders count on. If everything they told people to do was easy—drink, have many lovers, enjoy yourself—then no one would need them. If they tell people to do more difficult things—come to church, constantly pray, avoid excessive pleasure—then they're ramrods of rectitude.

And here's the big kicker that naturally follows this philosophy: If what you're doing is the true path, if the way you're living your life is the only sensible way to get to an orgasmic afterlife, then the way everyone else is doing it is wrong. Moreover, if they're doing it wrong, then they are probably being led on by an opposing force—you know, like the guy with the horns and the tail, what's his name, oh, yeah, the devil. And we all know what our moral duty is when confronted with the devil or with people being influenced by the devil.

Convert them or destroy them.

By destroying them—or, in less fatal terms, impugning their integrity, denying their rights, causing them harm—we earn points with the Great One; we're doing the Great One's work.

Again, some religious people do wonderful things on many levels; I know them personally. They're kind, they're generous, they lead others to be kind and generous. That's fine. But I'm pretty sure those people would be behaving in the same way regardless of their religion. You shouldn't have to rely on the Bible to do good in this world, particularly when plenty of people rely on it to do bad.

What's the upshot of all this? We have non-thinking, obeisant people carrying out extremely conservative policies laid down by autocrats trying to maintain authority. That doesn't bode too well for the rest of us, does it. We have people doing awful things who won't listen to reason. What could be worse?

Two tines down, one to go.

Chapter 4
The Dumb

The first tine of the Fork is greedy people who use their money to foist all sorts of hardships on those of who don't have as much money. The second tine of the Fork is ultra-religious people who will stop at nothing to ensure that their way of life supersedes all others'. Leaders of the first group buy converts, and leaders of the second group persuade converts to trade reason for obeisance. But what about members of the third tine, the dumb? How do they fit into this dystopia?

The dumb are critical to the Fork, for without this third tine there wouldn't be enough numbers for the other two tines to work their evil.

We've already talked about people who willingly give up their reasoning powers to buy into religious dogma. But there's another group out there—people who have *never* used reasoning powers, people who don't know *how* to use reasoning powers. These are people who are susceptible to certain kinds of persuasion.

Most of us know that correlation does not necessarily equal causation. That is, if a stork flies overhead just before a woman gives birth, it doesn't automatically follow that the stork brought the baby. If the unemployment rate dipped the same month as corporations got a tax cut, it doesn't automatically follow that tax cuts mean more jobs. And if your mother got over the flu immediately after you prayed for that to happen, it doesn't automatically follow that your prayers had any impact at all on her medical condition. Most of us know these things—but not all of us.

Most of us know that there are more than two sides to an issue. It's not that drinking milk is either good for you or bad for you. It's not that negotiating with a hostile country will either promote peace or discourage peace. It's not that a certain Senator is either honest or dishonest. Most issues are multilateral: You need to consider many factors, gather lots of information, and make nuanced judgments on them. Most of us know these things—but not all of us.

Most of us know that the source of information is often as important as the information itself. When a study about "The Health of Eating Peanuts" is financed by the American Peanut Growers Association, you should be wary of the study's findings. When multimillionaires say that the reason to register corporations offshore is to minimize red tape and not to avoid taxes, you should doubt their rationale. When Fox News reports anything, you should ignore it. People with vested interests in the information they put forth have an increased responsibility to prove the validity and reliability of that information. Most of us know these things—but not all of us.

So when I talk about "dumb," I'm not talking about being unable to name the capital of South Dakota (or even to know that it's pronounced "peer" and not "pee air"). I'm not talking about being unable to figure out the area of a rectangle. I'm not talking about being unable to describe the contributions to society of Albert Einstein, Edgar Allan Poe, or Margaret Sanger. What I am talking about is being unable to distinguish fact from fiction, logic from fallacy, thoughtfulness from bombast, and intellect from moronicity. Most of us can do this—but not all of us.

I give you the aforementioned Eve Wellington[1], second-grade teacher at Costa Via Public School, Albuquerque, New Mexico. I flew to Albuquerque to interview Ms. Wellington because of something she said that I found on-line. We talked in a classroom, and she was very friendly.

Me: "Ms. Wellington, you were recently quoted in the local paper as having said that you thought President Obama was a Muslim?"

Wellington: "Well, I guess he is. He's never denied it, and there's plenty of proof that he was in one of those, um, Muslim schools someplace in Asia, or Africa, where he grew up. Listen, if he had his way, we would be living under, what is it, Sharia law before my kids get old enough to vote. And then it would be too late. Hey, I believe in America, and everything I've seen says that he—Obama—doesn't."

Me: "Okay, but when you say there's plenty of proof, could you give me some examples? I mean, you must have some pretty strong reasons for saying that, right?"

Wellington: "Oh, I can't tell you the exact place I heard this, but I know I heard it from a bunch of places. The news. Yeah, I heard it on the news, and people were talkin' about it. I think I also read it in some magazine, I can't remember which one, but they had the dates and names and such of the schools he attended, and they had pictures, too. And pictures don't lie."

Me: *(pausing)* "Right. Pictures don't lie. So what else do you believe about President Obama, Ms. Wellington? Do you believe he was born in the United States?"

Wellington: *(snorting)* "Are you serious?"

Me: "Well, I—"

Wellington: "Of course he wasn't born in the United States! Oh, that's what the liberal media would want you to believe, but I think anyone with an open mind can see that the facts are different, you know? I mean, if someone like Donald Trump, with all his money and smarts and political know-how, if someone like him thinks that Obama is not a true American, then I think that tells you somethin' right there, now don't it."

Me: "Well, it certainly does; I think we're agreed on that. Ms. Wellington, I assume that you watch the news on TV, and you read, uh, magazines, and you probably listen to the radio. Are there other places you get information? Are there sources you seek out to check whether something is true or not?"

Wellington: *(pondering)* "Well, there's my fellow teachers; they're pretty smart. And there's a guy in the grocery—he's got a Ph.D., I think, and he always has opinions—and facts—about what's going on in the news. So, yeah, I ask around."

Me: "And what about your students?"

Wellington: "My students?"

Me: "I was just wondering if you talked to them about politics, or science, or anything like that."

Wellington: "Well, I think they're too young to understand politics and such, but they know basic science, of course, or at least they will after the end of this year. And they hear stuff from their parents, I'm sure. They know who Obama is. I don't know if they have an opinion about where he was born or what religion he preaches. I'm guessing that they follow their parents' opinion, just like everyone else."

Me: "And their teacher's opinion? Do you think they follow your opinion, too?"

Wellington: "Oh, sure. I'm absolutely certain that they were tickled pink when their parents told them that their teacher was in the paper. That's the first time for me, and I was pleased as all get-out to be quoted like that. I even had one of my kids ask me about it, and I told her. She wanted to know what Sharia law was. I told her she should ask her parents, but that it was pretty bad and that Obama wanted it. *(laughs)* You should have seen her expression. 'The President wants bad law?' *(laughs again)* Kids."

In this respect, the philosophy of the dumb is similar to the philosophy of the over-religious. It goes something like this:

"That person is different from me. That person is different from me because of (sex, sexual orientation, age, color, size, clothing style, haircut, ethnic background, nationality, religion, political affiliation, language, accent, traditions, diet, education, etc.). Therefore, that person is not as good as I am. And I will (avoid, hate, discriminate against, disparage, kill) that person."

Consider some of the results of a survey conducted by Survey Designs, Inc.[2], in April 2015. The respondents were a random selection of U.S. citizens aged 21 or older, and the items were constructed to avoid any overt religious implications:

- 35% believe that moon landings are a hoax.

- 45% don't believe in the concept of evolution.

- 57% don't believe that human behavior has a negative effect on the environment.

- 58% believe that homosexuality is a choice.

- 61% believe that they have had at least one past life.

- 63% believe that some people—e.g., astrologers, fortune-tellers, psychics—can see into the future.

- 65% believe that some people—e.g., religious leaders—can communicate directly with God.

- 66% believe that in the long run, whatever benefits the rich will benefit everyone else.

- 76% believe that in the long run, whatever foreign policies the United States carries out will improve the condition of the world.

That's more than scary; that's almost apocalyptic. Is it not a marvel that we're not in worse shape? The only consolation is that people this stupid are generally—not always, but generally—not in positions to influence millions of others.

They are, however, in positions to support people who are in positions to influence millions of others, and that's the big problem. If a campaign starts to dismantle the Environmental Protection Agency because, the campaign's proponents say, the environment doesn't need protection, dumb people will join that campaign. If a presidential candidate says that any kind of vaccine will cause more harm than good, dumb people will vote for that candidate. If a terrorist organization offers good pay, notoriety, respect, and unlimited sex after death, dumb people will volunteer to become martyrs for that organization.

These are not exaggerations. Teresa Crowder[3] blew up a clinic in Pittsburgh because, essentially, she's dumb. She'd watched a local "reality" TV show featuring the family of a seven-year-old boy. The boy had been seen at the George Foster Medical Center for a regular checkup and within a week had contracted an infection that eventually rendered him blind. The family testified on the show to their belief that a "booster" injection had caused the infection. Even the boy, when asked what he thought was the reason for his blindness, responded "Booster." The studio audience awwed on cue and then applauded. No medical professionals, either from the clinic or elsewhere, appeared, and apparently no medical professional was consulted. The host of the show said that "something needs to be done about clinics like these."

Crowder, the single mother of a seven-year-old boy and a five-year-old girl, could relate; she was incensed. She asked her boyfriend if he knew where she could "get a bomb." He did, she got one, and she left it in the women's room on the second floor of the clinic. It exploded, killing three people and wounding eight others. Teresa Crowder was videotaped by a security camera, tracked down, arrested, tried, convicted, and sentenced to prison for at least the next 20 years, as was her boyfriend. Her two children will no doubt receive better parenting in the future.

Mack Lee Johnson[4], 27, lived in Oklahoma City. He became convinced that the animals at the Oklahoma City Zoo were being mistreated. How was he convinced of that? He saw it on Facebook. They were being mistreated; they were confined to cages! We know this only because of Johnson's Facebook comments, one of which was "That zoo needs to go byby (sic), and I'm just the guy to do it." Johnson, a single man with two dogs and a cat, determined to rectify the situation. He snuck into the zoo one night and, with his experience as a mechanic, opened the cages of the lions, the bears, the gorillas, and the one alligator. As you might expect, he opened the cage of the lions last; they tore him to pieces. Before the animals were recaptured, they had wounded five other people. Johnson's two dogs and cat will no doubt receive better care in the future.

Of course, the dumb hurt themselves. The Darwin Awards regularly go to people who have died as a result of their own stupidity and therefore have no more opportunities to pass on their genes. And people do dumb things all the time: They shoot themselves while playing with a gun, they get run over by their own car while they're opening the trunk on a hill, they get electrocuted while trying to poke a bug in a wall socket with tweezers. But these people hurt others, too: They shoot bystanders while playing with a gun, they run over pedestrians while talking on a phone, and they set fire to apartment buildings because they try to relight a gas stove after the gas has been on.

Stupid decisions? Yes. And with most of these people, it's only a matter of time before they endanger themselves or others because of their poor judgment. The gun probably didn't go off the very first time they played with it; the fact that it didn't go off is probably reinforcement for playing with it again. The same goes for texting while driving and many other dimwitted actions.

But it's not these individual incidents that are the real problem, even though injury and death to innocents may occur. The real problem occurs on a grander scale.

We sometimes deride elected officials because we perceive them as stupid. We listen to their comments or their speeches, we read their policy statements or their books, we watch them perform at a state fair, and we think to ourselves, how in the world did this idiot get elected? And that leads to this truly depressing thought: This idiot got elected because thousands of dumb people voted for this idiot.

A famous experiment was carried out at the University of Michigan by Drs. Russell Floryn and Patricia Hayne and published in the December 1997 *Journal of Political Psychology*[5]. In the experiment, subjects were shown three videos of people running for mayor of a fictitious city and asked to choose the one they thought the most able. The experimenters varied the "candidates" to account for sex, race, and age, and they also accounted for those variables in the subjects.

Two of the candidates espoused policies that were boring but plausible: restructuring the amendment practices of the city council; requiring semi-monthly instead of monthly reporting from the police department; establishing a committee to look into how many trains passed through the city on a given day; changing the provider of salt for snow removal. These candidates occasionally looked down to consult their notes, stuttered a bit, and didn't wear makeup.

The third candidate espoused policies that were clearly nonsensical: requiring dogs to be leashed even inside houses; declaring that henceforth Sunday and Monday would be considered the weekend; restricting the paint color of downtown buildings to green, such restriction to be retroactive; shutting off all electricity for one day a month throughout the year as a way to conserve energy—even in hospitals; and requiring a dress code for anyone over 14, such dress code to be detailed in a pamphlet that would be forthcoming. This candidate spoke extemporaneously with linguistic flourishes, argued forcefully for the measures, wore flattering makeup, and had an ingratiating smile.

A slight majority of subjects—regardless of sex, race, and age—considered the third candidate—regardless of sex, race, and age—to be the most able. When asked for their reasons, they used phrases like "knew what she was talking about," "made sense," "seemed like a leader," and "was persuasive."

Professor Hayne, for one, wasn't surprised:

> We thought this might happen. We're sufficiently familiar with the literature to understand the power of presentation, as opposed to the impact of content. What did surprise me a little, however, was the lack of influence by sex or race. I would have thought that either of those would trump presentation, and maybe that's a good thing, that the subjects weren't sexist or racist.

I suppose that is a good thing, but the subjects were still—how shall I put it—intellectist.

In a sense, the results of this experiment should not astonish anyone who lives under the rule of a brain-challenged councilperson, mayor, state or federal representative, county executive, senator, governor, or president. Some of these officials are clearly mindless, but they do get elected, over and over again. True, some people might weigh policy over intelligence, and that may account for their votes—as well it should—but undoubtedly other people don't give intelligence any weight at all.

Readers may protest that the Dumb are different from the Greedy and the Over-Religious because they can't be responsible for the genetic limits of their intellect. One chooses to be greedy or over-religious, but one can't help being dumb. Developmentally disabled people shouldn't be castigated for their deficits.

Fair enough, except for two salient points. The first point is that many people—even "smart" people—use far less intellect than their genetic limits would indicate. Maybe they're lazy, maybe they have other priorities, maybe their emotional makeup obscures their mental makeup.

The second point is this: Whether willingly dumb or genetically handicapped, it doesn't really matter. When it comes to voting and to supporting campaigns, it's the *actions* that count, not the motivations. If a woman gives money to a congressional candidate who campaigns on bombing Mexico because she believes that Mexico is the cause of illegal immigration, I don't particularly care about the origin of her dumbosity; the effects are the same whether she's below that IQ line we consider developmentally normal or above it.

The question is not whether the Greedy, the Over-Religious, and the Dumb can help being that way; the question is what they *do*. If you want to amass a fortune by selling something people want, then fine; but when you abuse your employees or foist an unhealthy product on the public or use your money to promote dangerous policies, then you're a problem. If you believe that your god told someone to build an ark and gather pairs of animals into it while the earth was flooded, then fine again; but when you insist that public schools teach that in history class, then you're a problem. And if you pay serious attention to your horoscope every day and think that cancer can be cured by massage and remember being abducted by Martians, then I have no objections; but when you withhold medical services from your son because you think that homeopathy and reiki are more effective, then you're a problem.

It's the act more than the person.

Did we always have a problem with the greedy, the over-religious, and the dumb? Yes. But, I hear you say (there go those voices again), we have so many more opportunities these days to expose the tines of the Fork. Everyone outside the most primitive societies has access to communication channels now; there are so many different kinds of media— telephone, radio, television, the Internet and all its permutations. Why are we still getting forked when we have the means to inform people?

Ah, the media. We will address that next. Just remember, though, that the media are mere conduits. They are IV tubes in which all manner of liquids— toxins as well as antitoxins—can be infused into your mind. Luckily, you can almost always repel the toxins, but yanking out the IV tubes is a different matter indeed.

Chapter 5
The Media

These days, a message from one person can be transmitted within seconds to another person almost anywhere in the world. This message can be written, illustrated, photographed, spoken, coded, or filmed. The only thing faster or cleaner would be telepathy, and we probably have at least a few years before that becomes a reality.

There are many implications to this phenomenon. One is that so many more people can communicate with each other—exponentially more than ever before. Another is that not only can more people send messages, but also more people can receive them simultaneously. So I can send an Email only to my wife, and immediately after that I can send a Tweet to a million people I don't even know.

But a third implication is worrisome. There are essentially no filters on all this Internetic communication. Not that there should be—but that fact alone makes said communication potentially very dangerous. I can write a lie, doctor a photograph, record a fake speech, and film actors to persuade others to think or behave in a certain way. And we know that extremely hungry audiences are ready to be fed food that tastes good, whether or not it's healthy.

An early study of on-line communications was conducted by Social Psychologist Craig Kreidler of

Batchold University in Edmonton, Canada[1]. He found that on a given day, of messages that could be labeled as "true," "mostly true," "false," or "mostly false"—i.e., messages purporting to report on a factual occurrence—fully 38% fell into the latter two categories. Granted, this was not a comprehensive study, but the messages were as randomly generated as possible, and I'm willing to bet that that percentage jives with your own experience. I'm not talking about opinion statements, such as "Hillary Clinton is a terrible person"; I'm talking about statements of fact/fiction, such as "Hillary Clinton murdered her college roommate."

Last year, I formed a panel[2] consisting of a high school student, another high school student's mother and father, a political blogger, a print journalist, an advertiser for an energy company, and a small-town televangelist (When I initially described the topic of the discussion—the nature and impact of media on our lives—only the print journalist balked, and that was because he feared that print journalism was being unfairly targeted as an unreliable, out-of-date source of information. I assured him otherwise). I focused our discussion on the following questions (among others):

1. "How has the accessibility of so many different types of media affected the way you go about your daily life?"

2. "How do you distinguish what's true from what's not true?"

3. "How do you yourself use on-line social and political media to foster your own opinions?"

4. "What, if anything, would you like to see changed in the way we communicate these days?"

The entire discussion lasted about two hours. I'm going to give you excerpts from some of the responses. I'm not going to reveal the names of the panelists.

1. "How has the accessibility of so many different types of media affected the way you go about your daily life?"

Student: "I don't know; it makes it pretty cool, I guess, compared to what it used to be like. I can use my phone and get all the information I want."

Mother: "It's too much of a distraction. I can always find something on-line that's more fun than what I'm supposed to be doing."

Journalist: "Well, to be honest, it's jeopardizing the industry for which I've worked all these years. People are impatient. They don't want to go out and buy a newspaper or even have it delivered to their doorstep. That's too much trouble. They don't want to hold this huge thing in their hands while they thumb through the pages looking for the rest of the article they started. And they're not satisfied with print; they want videos. And one more thing: They want more volume, not just, say, 20 pages. Oh, and they want the ability to immediately share what they've just read. We can't do that with newspapers."

Advertiser: "It's made it easier and more difficult—easier because I have so many more avenues to tell people about us; more difficult because each of those avenues has its own rules and audience and ways to communicate. But on the whole, it's great. I have so many advantages over my counterparts from 20, 30 years ago. I can reach so many more people."

2. "How do you distinguish what's true from what's not true?"

Father: "For one thing, you check the source. Is this guy likely to be telling me the truth? No offense, *(name of advertiser)*, but I'm probably not going to accept as truth anything from someone trying to push something on me. That goes for politicians as well as admen."

Advertiser: "In my line of work, there's an easy answer, and I don't mean to be flippant about this: It doesn't matter. What matters is how well you send a message, whatever the message is. That's not to say that I'm lying all the time; far from it. But I have certain goals in my work, and I develop my message based on achieving those goals. So if you accept the premise of the goals—which I do—then everything else is mechanics."

Televangelist: "I *know* what's true. I can tell you're going to laugh at this, but God's word cannot be distorted in the eyes of true believers, no matter what kind of Internet program you're using. I'm not talking about facts, like how a Congressman voted or whatnot. I'm talking about the real truth behind a policy position or a product endorsement or even a comedian's monologue. I've trained myself to look for that inner truth, and in turn I share it with my own audience."

3. "How do you yourself use on-line social and political media to foster your own opinions?"

Student: "It's not that big a deal. My friends and I share what's on our mind. And if someone disagrees, that's fine; no problem. I mean, there's some people who are really abusive, but we just ignore them. And we can always block them. I don't know what the problem is."

Blogger: "Well, that's what I do, of course. I try to back up my opinions with facts, but it's not always the case. Sometimes it's just my opinion. And I put it out there, and I target audiences that I think will benefit from it, and I push it in as many ways as I can. I focus on those who are most likely going to agree with me, and on those who might be in the middle but who might be persuaded. I don't worry about the ones on the opposite side; it's usually not worth the energy to try to convert them."

Journalist: "I don't. I use the newspaper, which is probably why most people haven't heard of me." *(laughter)*

Advertiser: "Well, if by 'your own opinions,' you mean 'your company's opinions,' I use every tool that's available. I don't think you want me to get into the details, but let's put it this way: If the people I work for want to get a message out, they come to me, and I get that message out to everyone who needs to hear it, or see it. It's like shouting from a mountaintop so that everyone can hear you. No, it's better than that:

It's like shouting from a mountaintop so that everyone you *want* to hear you can hear you."

4. "What, if anything, would you like to see changed in the way we communicate these days?"

Mother: "I think we spend too much time on-line. I know that's an old statement, I mean, many people have said that, but it's true! When you talk on-line, it's just words, but you can't have the, I don't know what you call it, interplay, I guess. And even when you, uh, Skype? Is that it, Skype? Even when you Skype, it's not the same as being there. I think too many people are too suggestible—people that might question something if somebody was standing right next to them, but it's too easy to let something slide when you get a Tweet or an Email or you read a Post on Facebook. Pretty soon you're thinking like everyone else, because you haven't had time to really experience the person who's giving you the message and reflect on what that person said."

Father: "I know I'm old-fashioned about this, but I think that Tweets are not the greatest invention in the world. It's fine to be concise, but there are too many ways to misinterpret short little messages. At least with Email, you can write as much as you want. I'd like to see people take more time, be more thoughtful about what they write. Maybe, you know, the writing affects the thinking, and because people are so used to writing short, they start thinking short. I'm no scientist, I don't know if there's any truth to that or not, but stranger things have happened. Even if it's something as trivial as what you thought about a movie, can you really express all of that in a sentence or two?"

Blogger: "I'm actually pretty satisfied with the way things are turning out. Oh, I'd like to have more free access to more people, especially the movers and shakers, but I'm okay. There is a lot of competition, so maybe what I'd like to see changed is that it's harder for people other than me to blog."

Televangelist: "The Internet has become a haven for sinners. The most despicable language, the most sacrilegious, vile opinions are there for everyone to see. There need to be standards. There need to be qualifications for going on the Internet. I need a license to drive; why shouldn't I get a license to have access to millions of people? I can hurt many more people on the Internet than I can in my car. People can be swayed by devilish thoughts, and I fear for our welfare."

I present these excerpts to illustrate the point that some of us use media actively, while others are used by it passively. In that respect, it's no different from other forms of communication, but the significant difference is the sheer numbers. When they first appeared, radio, movies, and television all made a huge impact on how people received information, but not how they sent it. Telephones made a huge impact on how people conversed with one another, but generally—except for "party lines"—only two people at a time. The Internet favors both the senders and the receivers; it's your choice which you want to be.

Television and radio, of course, shouldn't be sold short. Some people live by what they see and hear on these two types of media. Everything a certain pundit might say is gospel to someone; if it wasn't, that pundit wouldn't be around for long. Just think about all the thousands of radio listeners who are duped very single year by April Fools jokes perpetrated by radio stations.

KCCY[3], a radio station in Klamath, Oregon, took the April Fools joke one step farther. They contracted with a "journalist" to offer editorials three times a week at the same time of the afternoon for three weeks— nine editorials in all. They gave him a fake name— Andrew Stack—and a fake background, and they said that he'd offer "non-mainstream" perspectives on the news. This differed from the University of Michigan experiment I cited earlier: In that experiment, candidates argued opinions and policies. In this instance, the radio personality offered "facts." Over the course of almost a month, "Andrew Stack" offered the following information, buttressed by a meandering logic and fallacious reasoning:

- One of the major components of the surface of the moon was indeed a type of cheese.

- Muslim terrorists in the Middle East carried miniature Torahs with them, "so they could always keep their enemy close at hand."

- Women are genetically predisposed to be less smart than men; this is almost entirely due to the fact that they are genetically predisposed to be shorter than men. The shortness in stature corresponds with a "shortness" in brain structure.

- Climate change exists, but it's the result of extraterrestrials tampering with our weather to see if we're sufficiently adaptable to meet with them.

- Three of the four Beatles were of African descent.

To be sure, people calling and Emailing in to KCCY put Stack down as a nutcase and wondered why the station was giving him air time. But many more—*many* more—people called and Emailed in to argue with Stack's pronouncements:

"Wouldn't cheese mold in space?"

"I've seen Torahs, and they're way too big for people to carry around with them. And miniature Torahs would be too small to read."

"If women are dumber than men because they're shorter, does that mean that short men are dumber than tall men? I've wondered about that because I know some people that that fits, but I don't know the science behind it."

"I don't believe in extraterrestrials. And I don't believe in climate change, either. This is just a ploy to take people's minds off real issues."

"John Lennon can't be black! He and all the other Beatles look even whiter than I do in their pictures!"

And so on. The radio listeners may have challenged Stack, but most accepted that there were grounds for his beliefs, no matter how outrageous.

Returning to the tines of the Fork, this is not good for you and me. Greedy corporate types can buy up tons of air time and foist their messages upon us. The dumb types will eat it up: The more the messages are swathed in sophisticated clothing, the more credible they'll be. Meanwhile, the over-religious take to the air to convince the dumb not only that their godly beliefs are true, but also that anyone diverging from those beliefs will be condemned to eternal damnation.

Now let's be fair: We can't check the credibility of absolutely everything that we see and hear; we can't even be sure of the credibility of those who claim to check the credibility of what we see and hear. Does that leave us two choices: believe everything or believe nothing?

Not quite. There is this thing called critical thinking. When we receive a message—a news report, an advertisement, an opinion—we *can* consider the sources of the information. We *can* check for internal consistency. We *can* look for signs of embellishment, of omission, of suggestion, of fallacious reasoning. We *can* check the other side—or, more likely, sides— of the argument, just to see if *that* makes more sense. At some point, we come to rely on a source, and then we don't check that source anymore. That's efficient, but it's not always wise. We need to be ever vigilant, as it is said, even among our friends.

From a 1524 missive[4] written by an English seaman to his brother (slightly modified to reflect modern-day linguistic usage):

People have sailed from our shores and some have not returned. Many of those who have returned tell horrific tales of monsters from the deep attacking their ships, tearing men in half, and ascending to the skies with their carcasses. We know from stories passed down from generation to generation that these creatures exist. Why would you doubt that these missing voyagers have met such a fate?

There you have it: tragic events, eyewitnesses, and research literature corroborating the existence of sea-and-air monsters. Maybe the corporate types back then profited from the purchase of monster-warning or monster-fighting equipment, so they were keen on preserving the veracity of the stories. Maybe the religious types back then profited from people committed to their way of life in order to get God on their side and protect them from such monsters, so they perpetuated the stories. And the dumb types would have eaten it all up.

Not only the dumb types eat it all up. We fought in Iraq based on information that couldn't possibly have been true. Most of America bought it. They considered the sources: mainly Republicans, but also some Democrats. They listened to the evidence, which was difficult to substantiate. They gave in to the emotions of patriotism and nationalism and anti-Islamism. They wanted revenge for the 9-11 attack. They wanted to err on the side of protecting ourselves. They thought, why would our president lie to us? It must be true.

We know where that went.

During the course of my research for this book, I crossed paths with the journalist Jane Goodson[5]. If the name is familiar, you may remember her for her 2009 exposé of the Carson Technical and Supply Company[6]—CTSC—which cheated the U.S. government out of millions of dollars while pretending to supply our troops overseas with food and other supplies. Goodson's series of articles, written for the Austin *Herald*[7], caused an uproar in many arenas, including Congress; CTSC was found guilty of fraud, and its case is likely to be under appeal for years to come.

But Goodson's story doesn't end there. She did receive several awards for her reporting, but, ironically, it became more, not less, difficult for her to continue in her chosen career. Over a series of lunches and lattés, the lanky, casually dressed 40ish woman with a friendly demeanor spoke as eloquently as she writes when she tried to explain what happened to her.

"It wasn't the editors, let me make that clear," she began. "It was me. It was all me. I wanted to maintain the momentum. I wanted to 'keep up my good work.' The problem was, journalism doesn't work that way. You can't create what isn't there. No, let me edit that: You *shouldn't* create what isn't there."

Although Goodson was praised, she was also criticized, and she took the latter to heart. It was said that her writing was occasionally too stilted. It was said that some people—the people she most wanted to reach—were struggling to understand her. Her words were too big, her sentences too long, her paragraphs and stories too convoluted.

So she decided to dumb it down—a lot. Over the next few years, she pursued five different projects, each of which was eventually rejected by her editors—not only of the *Herald* but also of two national magazines. Why was her work rejected?

"I went for the basics. I reduced the complexity to bare equations. I so desperately wanted to reach the hoi polloi that I'm afraid I betrayed everything I learned about journalism. I sacrificed accuracy for simplicity. Why should I explore the intricacies of environmental activism when instead I could portray the activists as white knights fighting aristocratic evildoers? Why should I spend hours constructing an analysis of our prison system when instead I could use one or two incidents to paint a picture of abuse? And why in the world would I interview professors who had no particular viewpoint about the collaboration of researchers and drug companies when it was far easier to talk with people who had something to gain or lose from my reporting?"

She sighs.

"Luckily, I had editors who had higher standards than I did. It took me all this time to get back on track, and I'm still not where I was."

Other writers aren't so lucky; they have editors who are only too happy to go with the facile headline, the slanted interview, and the black-and-white tale of wrongdoing. If there's sex, violence, or political scandal involved, all the better. And that plays into all three tines of the Fork. It gives an opportunity for the greedy to claim unwarranted persecution; it gives an opportunity for the over-religious to point to the sinfulness of humanity; and it gives an opportunity for the dumb to claim they know what's going on when they don't.

And let us not forget: Some media outlets purposefully distort the facts. There, I said it. If you're the head of one of these media outlets, and if you bring in readership, listenership, viewership, and—most importantly—advertising revenue from a certain base, then you can slant everything to that base. You may even hire employees who belong to that base, so they seem as sincere as possible. And you do this because you probably belong to either the first or second tine of the Fork—or both: You do this to make money, you do this to reaffirm your zealous religious beliefs, or you do this to make money while reaffirming your zealous religious beliefs. And you reel in other members of the Fork. Who needs to think when the news host has already done the thinking for me?

So what can we do? How can we protect ourselves from the nuances and the exaggerations and the outright lies that some of the media sell us?

I know! We can teach people how to be critical thinkers! And what better place to do that than in our schools?

Chapter 6
Schools

In 2011, University of Edinborough professors Anita Lasseter and Thomas Payne interviewed 220 people in the United Kingdom between the ages of 25 and 40.[1] They wanted to learn about school experiences: what they were, how they were received, and to what extent they were helpful in later life—or at least between the ages of 25 and 40. They were interested in academic as well as social experiences, and the results I want to call attention to relate to classwork that involved critical thinking, which in the study was defined as "the ability to distinguish fact from fiction, to use logic, to avoid fallacies, and to make reasonable attributions and judgments based on reliable information":

- Nineteen percent of respondents indicated that they received some kind of classroom experience involving critical thinking.

- Forty-three percent of respondents indicated that they think more classroom experience involving critical thinking would have helped them in their professional lives.

- Twenty-eight percent of respondents indicated that they think more classroom experience involving critical thinking would have helped them in their personal lives.

- Eighty-nine percent of respondents indicated that they were critical thinkers.

Now, on the face of it, you might think, oh, that's good; these folks are critical thinkers despite the lack of any substantial instruction in that topic. They're mostly satisfied with the instruction they did get, and everything's just dandy.

Except it's not: Before the interviews, Lasseter and Payne gave all the subjects "critical thinking tests"—little problem situations to which they had to respond in several ways. Their responses were measured based on the extent to which they used critical thinking.

With 100 being "exceptional use of critical thinking" and 0 being "lack of any critical thinking," the subjects scored a dismal average of 31. Clearly, people thought they were using their brains when they weren't.

To my knowledge, this study has yet to be duplicated in the United States, but I'd hazard a guess that if it were, the average would be about the same. And why wouldn't it? Do you recall any classes in critical thinking? Did you participate in debates when you were in high school or college, in which you had to argue both sides of a question? Did you write "critical" essays of pieces of literature and have to defend those essays or argue against others' essays? Were you taught anything about logic or fallacies? Don't you think some of those experiences might have been helpful when listening to a radio shock jock talk to you about the Middle East or a local politician lecture you about the economy?

Why in the world would critical thinking be so much lower on the academic curriculum than geometry or meteorology or Old English literature? For that matter, why is it perfectly okay to compel students to take physical education classes so they can exercise their body but not critical thinking classes so they can exercise their mind?

Let's take an example: The owner of a restaurant refuses to seat two gay men. He knows they're gay because they're holding hands when they enter the restaurant, because they "look gay," and because one of them utters stereotypically gay things like "oh, please" and "will you shut right up now" when quasi-arguing with his companion.

Now, someone might say, hey, it's his restaurant, he should be able to seat or to kick out anyone he wants. Moreover, if the concept of homosexuality is against his religion, our constitution protects his right to exercise that religion, and to serve these people would be tantamount to aiding and abetting a mortal sin.

Well, there are a lot of things wrong with that position, and critical thinking would enable you to identify those things. For example, if as owner of the restaurant he's able to seat or to kick out anyone he wants, that means he could kick out African-Americans, right? And Jews? And blind people? And people with accents? And people who were wearing the color blue?

Critical thinking might lead you to consult the U.S. Constitution to see if it lets an individual exercise a religion in a public establishment to discriminate against individuals. You'd find that it doesn't.

And critical thinking might make you wonder this: If you're guided only by your religion, and you act based upon what your religion considers a mortal sin, then what are the limits? Maybe my religion states that people over 65 years old should be put to death. Maybe my religion states that women should be sexually available to anyone who desires to have sex with them. Maybe my religion states that people who take my deity's name in vain should be burned alive.

Nonsense? Not really. What's good for one religion should be good for another, no matter how inane, right? But that's why we have separation (though not nearly enough) of Church and State in this country: Church rules are entirely arbitrary. And in most cases they're immutable. And they must be unquestioned. How can a multicultural society exist under those rules?

Critical thinking means that you don't automatically accept the norm. Here's a norm: What's good for business is also what's good for the country. You can see that, can't you? Acme Industries makes millions of dollars selling anvils. The demand for anvils rises, so Acme Industries hires more people. More profits equals more demand equals more employment. Right?

Not always. First of all, just because Acme's sales are doing well doesn't mean that they need more employees. The profits may go to the CEO or to the shareholders or to a new Acme plant overseas, where wages are a lot lower. Second of all, even if they do hire more people, it doesn't mean that they're going to pay them a fair wage or provide them with decent working conditions. And third of all, even if they did hire more people and pay them a fair wage and provide them with decent working conditions, it doesn't mean that they should be exempt from taxes or from environmental oversight or from fair trade practices.

It's like this: We generally don't have enough time to scrutinize every message we receive, whether that message is on Facebook or Twitter or the radio or TV or a pamphlet or from a conversation with a friend. At first glance, it seems reasonable that owners of restaurants should be able to serve whomever they please and that more money for businesses means more employment. But after the first glance, a lot of these positions falter, and some disintegrate. Issues are complex. They have more than two sides. For example, the question isn't "Should we ban guns?" It's more like "What are the consequences of banning guns?" What are the consequences of not banning guns?" "Which guns should we ban?" "Who should have access to guns?" "Under what circumstances should people have access to guns?" "What should the punishment be for using guns illegally?" "How can we most efficiently and effectively present and implement this policy?" "What else should we consider?"

In addition to the merits—or demerits—of a particular argument, who's making it? People are often remiss in not considering the source of an argument, or in some cases "over-considering" the source. Is the person objective? What in the person's circumstances might bias a judgment? Not all journalists are reliable. Not all university studies are legitimate. In both a meta-review of peer-reviewed studies and an experiment measuring people's responses to such studies, Sandra Bethune of Northwestern University determined that fully 88% of subjects considered a university-cited study "valid."[2] As a side note, she also found that almost an identical number—84%—didn't even bother to check the citations, because, as one sophomore reasonably said, "I wouldn't have time to look up all the footnote sources, anyway, so what's the point?"

Jane Carl[3] is a fifth-grade teacher at Fillmore Elementary School in Key Pines, Pennsylvania. She's an exceptional teacher—embraced by her students, admired by her colleagues, lauded by her principal. One of the things that make her exceptional is her devotion to teaching some form of critical thinking. She doesn't do this as a separate part of a lesson plan; rather, she incorporates critical thinking into virtually everything she teaches.

"So," she says, "if I'm teaching something about science, I'll always ask them questions like 'How do we know this is true?' or 'How could we check to see if this is true?' I'll do the same thing with, I don't know, punctuation. I teach them the rules, of course, but I'll also get them to talk about the rules. Like, 'Why do you think we need a semicolon here? What does the semicolon do that the comma doesn't do?' Or maybe, let's see, do you know what the Oxford comma is? Sure you do. So I'll give them a sentence and ask them if they think it needs an Oxford comma. Sometimes they'll argue with each other, which I think is great. I encourage that. It helps them learn each other's viewpoints, and often it strengthens their own viewpoints."

When I ask her students what they think of Ms. Carl, they're all complimentary, but they really can't articulate why they like her, which, given that they're mostly 9- and 10-year-olds, isn't surprising. One student, though, a little boy named Joseph, says something that strikes me as very interesting. When I ask him what is one thing that makes Ms. Carl different from other teachers he's had, he thinks for a moment and then says, "She likes fighting."

"She likes fighting." Is that true of critical thinkers? Do they prefer to fight rather than accept something at face value? Do they take pleasure in tearing something apart, particularly if that something is held dearly by someone else?

It may be true for some people. But for me, it's more of a choice: Fighting isn't the goal; it's the means to the end of finding the truth and making sure that everyone knows that truth, or at least knows that the truth isn't currently accessible. And if the question is whether to fight or to accept, then the choice is an easy one.

That doesn't mean that critical thinkers always fight. If the issue is a trivial one, or if it's simply one they don't care about, then critical thinkers will no doubt readily accept what's on the plate. But in other cases, the plate goes back to the kitchen.

So how do we teach this? Don't teachers have enough to do without being responsible for yet another curriculum, a curriculum that may not have any relationship at all to the tests that students have to take in high school and college?

The answer is the Jane Carl method: Incorporate critical thinking into *all* school curricula.

Here are some examples, and the appropriateness of these depends in large part on the grade of the student and the expertise of the teacher:

- In science, ask students to offer reasons why we're likely or not likely to be visited by extraterrestrials in the next 200 years. Have them argue both sides.

- In history, ask students how interpretations of events that happened 50, 100, and 500 years ago influence how we think today. Give examples such as the "discovery" of America by non-Natives.

- In language arts, ask students to identify fallacies, exaggerations, unattributed sources, other leaps of logic, and outright lies in political and other public statements. Be sure to discuss the reasons behind the misstatements.

- In geography, ask students how a country's terrain, its proximity to sea and ocean, and the nature of its neighbors contribute to its stability. Be sure to talk about present as well as past circumstances.

- In art, ask students why they think some forms of art are offensive to people. Create scenarios in which people might be offended by, say, toes or long hair.

- In math, ask students to discuss the extent to which they think it's important to learn geometry, trigonometry, algebra, and calculus. Be ready to provide rationales for each.

These exercises don't need to be graded, even though they may be the most useful activities in which students may participate. What these exercises do is stimulate those parts of the brain that address problems, that respond to others' statements and behaviors. These exercises expand students' ability to try to make sense of the world, to try to find the truth. It's not called *critical* thinking for nothing.

As an essential complement to the exercises, teachers—and administrators and other school staff— need to *model* critical thinking. In their discussions with students, they need to show that everything isn't a given, that it's perfectly okay to ask reasonable questions, and that young people won't be punished for challenging others' statements. Students might not always get a response that satisfies them, but that's okay.

And none of this needs to stop at high school graduation. Be honest: Wouldn't you consider a college course in Critical Thinking something valuable to sign up for? If you thought about it, regardless of your major, wouldn't you figure that critical thinking skills would help you for the rest of your life—in choosing a career, in choosing a romantic partner, in deciding whether and when to become part of a family, in joining a group, in accepting a job offer, in managing your money, in making health decisions? Shouldn't Critical Thinking be a required course in all universities?

Einstein once said, "The most important thing I learned in school was not what to think, but how to think."[4] And on possibly the other end of the scale, 1990's pop idol Julie Stevens[5] both sang and reiterated in interviews, "I went to school, felt like a fool; how I wish they'd opened my head."

Teaching critical thinking in schools isn't the answer to everything; there will still be awful people getting elected and absurd memes floating about and needless death and destruction being caused for a variety of reasons. But even a minor shift in the direction of helping young people think better is bound to help us.

In his 2005 book, *The Heart Leads*, Joshua Willis,[6] a past Methodist minister and current professor of political science, makes several telling points about critical thinking, and not necessarily favorable ones, either. One of them, from his chapter on the merits of religion, contains the following quote:

> You don't give up your humanity when you go to church. You embrace it. You accept a version of reality that may or may not be true, but you set aside your mind and substitute your heart. Not everything in this world is facts and figures. Sometimes you have to let go and rejoice in the mysteries of life.

It's not only Christians who feel this way. One of the most quoted passages[7] from the Koran—translated—is this:

Close your eyes to the here and open them to the everywhere.

And, fittingly, in the U.S. Army Manual for Recruits (Version 5)[8], you can find the following statement:

Obey your commanding officer without question or hesitation. No matter what you think, no matter what you fear, you must obey your commanding officer. This is a cardinal rule.

In all these cases, the rationale for the cessation of critical thinking is the same: Obeisance rules. You obey your commanding officer because, presumably, in the heat of battle your critical thinking might endanger yourself and others. You obey religious precepts because, presumably, when people start questioning religious rules or tales or traditions, the tent folds and the show stops.

But what about, as Willis says, "the mysteries of life"? Shouldn't we be less hard-assed and instead take it easy on occasion? Shouldn't we use our right brain at times and laugh and cry and be struck with awe and experience all of the emotions that are available to us?

The answer is yes. These feelings are not contradictory to critical thinking. We can appreciate the beauty of a Catholic Easter ceremony as much as a Mozart concerto. We can be absorbed by the story of David and Goliath as much as by the story of Don Quixote. We can decide to observe a religious Christmas as well as a secular Thanksgiving. And we can decide to join the Army and leave everything up to our commanding officers.

The point is that we don't disable our critical thinking; we leave it on low in the background. We belong to a church until the church starts telling us to do something horrible to others. We listen to everything our favorite politicians say until what they say starts conflicting with what we know to be true. We buy a certain product or use a certain service until the company that makes that product or provides that service crosses one of our ethical lines.

Critical thinking doesn't make us impervious to the effects of the Fork. But more people thinking more critically would certainly blunt the tines. And the place to encourage that critical thinking is school. It's just a shame that schools don't seem to have that as a priority.

It's not all a downer, though. People do exist in all forms of life who combat the Fork—in their own ways. Now you're going to meet some of them.

Chapter 7
Exemplars

Some people are fighting the Fork. Either they're dulling the tines or they're helping others repel the tines. Cases in point:

Sandy Chavez's official title is Executive Assistant, Development, but that doesn't even begin to describe what she does, how she does it, or what tremendous benefits she's achieved from her efforts. She works for Travis Industries, Inc., a company you've probably never heard of based in Cincinnati, but a company whose worth is valued at over $11 billion.[1]

Travis Industries makes uniforms and the accoutrements to those uniforms. It outfits military forces in the U.S. and elsewhere (only allies, though), police departments, fire departments, and organizations such as the Boy Scouts and Girl Scouts. It produces belts and holsters and epaulets and padding and just about everything else associated with uniforms. It's been in business since 1972, and it's done very well for itself. If you don't recognize the name of the company, it's because its founder and CEO, Chandler Travis, prefers to keep a low profile.

That is, he did until three years ago, when Sandy Chavez came on board.

Sandy Chavez grew up in Los Angeles, the daughter of Mexican immigrants. She was always a "do-gooder"—helping out neighbors, organizing fund drives, donating food and clothing. She also had a knack for business, though she never went to business school; instead, she earned a Masters in Social Work from UC-Berkeley and proceeded to work in corporations where she could put her do-goodness to use. In time, she came to Travis Industries. Within a year, she was well-known in the company and was brought to the attention of Chandler Travis, who, after several interviews and a project that allowed employees to donate their sick time to fellow employees in crisis, made Chavez his assistant.

Chavez got to work.

First she enlisted the cooperation of the company's CFO to reprioritize Travis Industry's holdings so that its money wasn't tied up in Big Oil or other environmental threats. At the same time, she worked with the company's Human Resources and Employment departments to improve working conditions at not only the headquarters in Cincinnati but also branches in Akron, Philadelphia, and Newark. Finally, she offered several suggestions to Development that enabled them to cast a wider and simultaneously more focused net on potential funders—funders that represented more of a progressive outlook.

The first year was tough. Although Chavez had essentially received carte blanche from Travis, others did not automatically follow her lead, and she had quite a few struggles, particularly with the financial executives. Nonetheless, after a year, the bottom line wasn't any worse—though no better—and by that time Chavez had managed to gain some important friends up and down the corporate ladder.

Her arguments—first to Travis and then to the other company leaders—went like this: Upper management at Travis is making good money. Travis Industries is making good money. It's time to give back. We can give back in three ways: One, we can make life better for our employees in terms of their pay and their surroundings. This will benefit us because they will become more satisfied with their work, more loyal to the business, and more productive. Two, we can donate some of our products to noble causes, for example, play uniforms for children in hospitals or firefighting uniforms for volunteer firefighters in impoverished communities. This will benefit us because it will generate good publicity and potentially more customers. And three, we can invest our money and our efforts in causes that may not have anything to do with our product but that help people and the environment. We should do all these things because they're the right things to do and because we're able to do them.

Chandler Travis was sold on this philosophy. As he said in a *Business Weekly* interview:

> She (Chavez) made me see something that I should have seen way a long time ago: I had a responsibility to do good. It's that simple. Now, what I see as doing good and what someone else sees as doing good may be different, but that's okay. The important thing is that people are benefiting from my actions, and that feels really fine.[2]

As for Chavez, she couldn't be happier, and she gives a lot of credit to Travis:

> It's all him. Really. I could talk till I'm blue in the face about what the company should do, where it should put its money, how it should treat its employees, but unless the top guy says okay, nothing happens. Mr. Travis deserves all the credit. He trusted me, someone he didn't know for very long. He has it in him, the same feelings that I do, and all I did was show him a way that he could make those feelings, you know, concrete. And he took a risk; he took a big risk. And I hope he feels good about it. I think he does.[3]

Sandy Chavez, Chandler Travis, and other decision-makers at Travis Industries have blunted the corporate tine of the Fork; they've shown that just because you have a lot of money doesn't mean that you can't do good.

Humanists for an Open and Progressive Environment—HOPE—is a nonprofit organization[4] that began in 2009; it was founded by Neal (yes, I'm biased) Occles[5] of Atlanta. Today it consists of 49 chapters in 11 states and claims over 1,500 members. Its purpose is threefold: to promote programs and policies that further an "open and progressive environment"; to combat programs and policies that would hinder an open and progressive environment; and to provide a forum for people to exchange ideas. Members of HOPE have successfully brought about the enactment of anti-discrimination and separation-of-church-and-state laws in Atlanta and Macon, Georgia; in Frankfort, Kentucky; in Jacksonville, Florida; and in Jefferson City, Missouri. They have helped to defeat repressive legislation in Macon; in Richmond, Virginia; in Clarion, Pennsylvania; and in the state of North Carolina. Volunteers lobby, organize, recruit, and offer editorials to local media.

Neal Occles grew up as the son of Southern Baptists, but clearly whatever it was that resonated with his family, friends, and neighbors never sat well with him. A couple of years ago, an Atlanta PBS station aired a documentary about him, "The Rebel,"[6] and I'm going to quote from that. Here's Occles on his early years:

> There was always something wrong. I think the first thing that hit me was the exclusionary policies of the church. There were so many bad people: They didn't like sodomites, whoever they were, though at the time I had the feeling they were talking about gay people, but I wasn't sure. For a while, I thought there was a country named Sodom, and these were immigrants or something. Anyway, they really didn't seem to like females, either. Females were treated way differently from males. And don't even think about hanging out with people who didn't believe the way they did. That was the worst, because

those people were sinners and going straight to hell. I guess maybe you might get caught in the downdraft or something and get sucked down with them. It was all so negative.

And then there were the Bible stories. I remember, I must have been very young, sitting in a pew between my mother and father, and the preacher would be talking about, I don't know, something horrible, like God killing a bunch of people because of some reason or other, and I shuddered at it, and I looked to my mother for comfort, and she was smiling! Smiling and nodding! *(shakes head)* I think it was at that moment I realized that this was a world I did not want to be part of. And, unfortunately, that was probably the beginning of a break between me and my parents that has never been . . . well . . . it's still there. The break is still there.

Occles tried to engage his parents in discussion, but he soon learned that that was not a fruitful endeavor: Questioning the Lord's word—or even the preacher's word—was not to be tolerated. He eventually kept his mouth shut, bided his time, and went through the motions of being, if not a devout churchgoer, at least an obedient son. Nor was it practical to talk about his alienation with his friends. The one time he tried that—at a sleepover, no less— he was ratted out and given a stern lecture by, in turn, his friend's parents, his own parents, and a representative from the church.

Occles graduated high school, went to college at Emory, and started his first HOPE chapter on campus. There he found students who had similar experiences:

> It was such a relief! There were actually people who thought like me! People who thought the Bible stuff was absurd! People who thought that the things we were taught in church and at home were horrible! Everybody felt it. It was like, like, you know, if you're different somehow—if you're black or disabled or, I don't know, a dwarf or something, you know, whatever—and you find people like you for the first time, it's just so—so liberating. That's how it was at Emory. Not only did we find each other, but we found a cause that together we could work toward. It was the high point of my life to that time, no doubt.

Occles used the acronym HOPE in part because he wanted to counter some of the attitudes that characterized many of the new organization's members: They'd been beaten down and were discouraged. Occles realized they needed a positive attitude to accomplish anything, and HOPE was just the vehicle to give that to them.

Occles earned a B.A. from Emory and an M.B.A. from the University of North Carolina. He lives in Raleigh and works for a management consultant company. HOPE is going strong: Occles does outreach all over the country, and was recently invited to speak in London and in Canberra, Australia, about his organization. Some of the activities put on by HOPE have included the following:

- facilitating "True Gospel" conferences, in which participants are shown how Bible passages can be applied to progressive causes

- enlisting humanistic religious leaders to meet with state members of the Congress and Senate about relevant upcoming legislation

- holding "Run for Justice" events, usually 10K runs, which act as fund-raisers as well as generators of publicity

- sponsoring "No-Sinner Dinners," which offer free food to people off the street without asking them anything about God or religion

Neal Occles resisted the second tine of the Fork. He didn't succumb to religiosity but instead produced an alternative, one that is gaining adherents every day.

Twins, even when they're not identical, often have strong bonds between them, and so it was with Arnold and Phyllis Berger[7]. Growing up in a middle-class home on Long Island, they didn't want for anything in particular, and they certainly didn't want for conversation: They were constant companions, engaged in constant dialog. They didn't always agree, but they were always civil.

Arnold and Phyllis grew up political: Mr. Berger was an alderman, and Mrs. Berger wrote a "what's-doing-around-town" column for the local newspaper, which doesn't sound political but sometimes ended up that way. The children engaged their parents around dinner on the topics of the day, and early on they became aware of the lies, nuances, pressures, influences, strategies, tactics, hypocrisies, and honest efforts of people in the public arena.

But the young Bergers grew up not as cynics, which might have been expected, but as truth-seekers, which was much more useful. Their three other siblings, as well as (later on) their parents, routinely came to them for their analyses of the latest political machinations or media story. Soon they garnered a reputation for such insight, and neighbors also sought their advice. This trend continued in school until 11th grade, when Phyllis got an idea.

"We were getting more and more depressed," she told me several years later in a conference call with her and Arnold (who at the time was on a road trip through Connecticut and spoke from a motel), "because the shoddy news reports never seemed to stop. Well, let me correct that: *I* was getting more and more depressed. Arnold's always been the glass-half-full partner."

"It's true," said Arnold. "Where Phyllis was getting depressed, I was being buoyed by all the people continually asking us to interpret the news for them."

"That's when I got the idea to make everything available to anyone who wanted it," said Phyllis.

Thus was born Dissect This!, a website (www.dissectthis.com)[8] on which Arnold and Phyllis not only interpret the most recent and important national speeches, press releases, and highlights from other websites, but also field requests (for $15 each) to interpret local speeches and press releases, for example, an Arizona congressman's claim that his proposed legislation would benefit the poor, or the statement put out by the mayor of Graveling, Iowa, indicating his displeasure with President Obama's foreign policy.

Phyllis: "It's not so much about disproving lies, though there's plenty of that to go around. But there are a lot of websites that fact-check. What we do is more, well, dissection. We say, look what he's doing here. He's painting with a broad brush, or he's attributing a general set of behaviors to one instance—"

Arnold: "Or the reverse. He—or she—might take a general trend and erroneously conclude that someone might act this way or that way."

Phyllis: "It's all manipulation."

Arnold: "Well, that's part of it. Some of it's manipulation, but a lot of it—well, at least *I* think a lot of it; I don't think Phyllis agrees—may be unintentional. People think in weird ways, and they seek out information to justify their conclusions. While we can't stop the politicians from doing that, maybe we can stop some of the voters from doing that, or at least get them to recognize that not everything politicians say makes sense—even the politicians they like."

Phyllis: "And we help them recognize *why* it doesn't make sense. That's the most important. Once they recognize what's happening, they can recognize it when it happens again—you know, see the pattern. Well, that's what we hope, anyway."

Since its debut a year and a half ago, Dissect This! has fielded 17,456 requests, and it's also offered the same number of analyses based on what the twins deem newsworthy. They've compiled their standard analyses into a handbook, which they sell for $9.95, and they're thinking of writing a full-fledged book on both their analyses and their experiences with Dissect This!

Arnold and Phyllis Berger aren't making dumb people smart. And they've probably made only an infinitesimal dent in the populace that believes, for example, that Glenn Beck remotely knows what he's talking about. But they have made an impact on how some people take in news and information. They have influenced how people respond to what they hear today and what they might hear tomorrow. And they have addressed the third tine of the Fork by giving people valuable tools to become good citizens.

So, progress is being made. We have Sandy Chavez, Neal Occles, and Arnold and Phyllis Berger all providing armor for people to defend themselves from getting forked. And many more exemplars exist—some on the local level, others on the state or national level. You have to know where to look.

Is there anything that these exemplars have in common? We can find commonalities in any group of people, to be sure, but perhaps these stand out:

They have a desire to improve the human condition.

They know their goals will meet obstructions, and they devise ways to overcome those obstructions.

They secure support from like-minded individuals, whether or not those individuals at the time know they are like-minded.

They persist through setbacks and frustration.

I now want to present "a better situation"—not a utopia by any means, but a modest vision that we may aspire to. After all, it's one thing to batter and bemoan the awfulness of what we currently endure; it's quite another to offer a viable alternative. That's what's next.

Chapter 8
A Better Situation

The Fork—the corporatists, the religionists, the no-brainists—is hurting us. It hurts us economically, environmentally, emotionally, and in other ways too numerous to mention. It has sent us to war, deadened our feelings of empathy, and condemned millions to lives of misery. We can do better. We have to do better.

I'd like to see changes in each of the three tines of the Fork. I'd like to see structural changes and psychological changes. This vision—the destruction or at least the severe blunting of the Fork—won't come easily.

But we have to start somewhere, so imagine this:

Tine 1, The Greedy: Structure

- Businesses' contributions to political campaigns are limited and transparent. Businesses contribute to a candidate or cause only after getting majority acquiescence from employees as well as stockholders.

  Constitutional law expert Dr. Sidney Trenton[1], University of Virginia: "It would no doubt require some previous court judgments to be overturned, but I believe there is ample precedent—and ample cause—for setting restrictions on businesses in this way."

- Businesses maintain vertical equity. In general, the top executive doesn't make more than 100 times what the lowest wage-earner makes. If the lowest wage-earner brings in $20,000 a year, then the top executive doesn't bring in more than $2,000,000 a year. Moreover, stockholders' dividends are limited by employees' wages.

  Currently, the average difference between the top executive and the lowest wage-earner in the top 25 U.S. corporations is 100,000%[2].

- Businesses are held accountable for civil rights and environmental transgressions. Inspections occur regularly and frequently. Whistle-blowers are protected. Defendants are brought to trial within a year. Penalties are paid within another year.

  Manhattan civil rights attorney Danielle Fromm[3]: "Justice is routinely delayed for defendants bringing cases against huge corporations. It might be years before the case comes to trial, and literally decades before penalties are paid, if ever."

- All U.S. businesses are headquartered within the U.S. and pay local, state, and federal taxes.

  U.S. Representative Charles Doctoring (D, Cal.)[4]: "It's a great concept, but the legislation would never pass. Too many people would lose too much money. Corporations would go under."

Tine 1, The Greedy: Psychology

- Businesses focus more on contributing to society. They routinely set aside a portion of net profits for a variety of causes—food for the needy, research into diseases, education for poor children, measures to protect and replenish the environment.

- Businesses consider human factors as part of any decision, e.g., to take over a company, to ship a toxic substance, to produce a harmful product, to allocate funds.

We will never rid people of the desire to make more money; too many people see that as the primary purpose of life. Even altruists want to make more money so they can give it to people who need it more. The issue isn't so much whether people should make a lot of money as it is how people should make a lot of money and what unfair privileges money gives them.

Economist of the 1940s and 1950s Charles Ruppert Morgens[5] put it well when he sounded a warning about the post-war boom in the U.S. and other countries:

> Economics is very complex. I don't want to alarm people about the extent to which they will earn or lose money over the next decade, and, frankly, things are looking good. What concerns me is the

nature of the people who are earning exorbitant amounts of money. Are they taking unfair advantage of others? Will they use this advantage to make more money and take even more unfair advantage of others? Wealth is a temptation, perhaps the greatest temptation. And man sees what he wants to see. We need controls. We need to prevent disaster. We need to protect those who cannot see what may befall them.

Morgens was clearly prescient, though the clues have always been there. Corporations have forever been ruthless. The unions helped immensely, but if you're a certain type of corporate executive, your philosophy is the traditional one: Make money any way you can. And continue to make money any way you can. What that means in concrete terms is to disregard the welfare of your employees, ignore the effects your work may have on the environment, market your world-view to any audience who will listen, and ceaselessly lobby elected officials to enact legislation favorable to your company.

It's not that all corporate executives are evil; not at all. But as Morgens pointed out, wealth is a temptation, and we shouldn't automatically assume that what's good for the company is good for everyone.

Tine 2, The Over-Religious: Structure

- Churches and religious organizations enter partisan politics at their peril. As soon as any religious organization—church, synagogue, ashram, school, etc.—contributes money to a partisan campaign or otherwise strays across the religion/state line, that organization relinquishes its "religious" category and pays federal, state, and local taxes based on its income for the next five years, at which point it can appeal to be reinstated as a religious organization.

Mark Rampling, pastor, First Presbyterian Church, Seaworth, Oregon[6]: "A church can't have it both ways. It can't pretend to be apolitical but actually be political and then claim, no, you can't tax us. It is the church's duty to tend to God's matters, not politics. Where religious entities cross the line, they should pay the penalty."

- Being a member of a church or religious organization does not exclude obeying local, state, and federal laws, whether civil or criminal. Members may be charged with sex discrimination, race discrimination, sexual orientation discrimination, vandalism, property infringement, default on debts, and other infractions.

Tine 2, The Over-Religious: Psychology

- All religions are explicitly acknowledged as depending on fiction for their beliefs. Noah's ark, the Garden of Eden, a virgin birth, angels, miracles, a resurrection, life after death, heaven and hell, and an omniscient, omnipotent, supernatural deity—all those beliefs and more are considered on a par with beliefs in Poseidon's mastery of the sea, in Martians having created humans, in leprechauns, in gnomes, in elves, in flying spaghetti monsters, and in other stories and characters. People still refer to "holy books," but they regard them as containing cautionary tales and metaphors.

- No religion considers itself the one with the only true beliefs. All people tolerate others with different beliefs. Whereas the motto for any religion might have been "This is the one and only true word," now it is "This works for me, for now."

- Religious organizations tend to those who are poor and needy, who are without homes or jobs, who are stricken with disease, and who are otherwise hurting physically or emotionally. This service is their *raison d'etre*; adherents realize that their mission on earth is to do good works.

In terms of effecting change, this may be the most difficult tine. You can try to reason with greedy people, and you can try to educate ignorant people, but with the over-religious, well, reason is not the currency in which they deal. If people from the Church of the Right believe that left-handed people are evil and that they should not have the same access to jobs, health care, or public services, then showing those people how illogical their beliefs are will not be persuasive: "It says in the Book of the Righteous that 'Left-handed ones are the scourge of the earth and should be expelled from human society.' There is no argument here."

Religion makes people abuse others; think of the Crusades. It makes people abuse themselves; think of Islamic martyrs who fly jets into skyscrapers. Conversely, it gives them freedom—freedom from thinking, making decisions, considering consequences, and accepting responsibility. What a deal!

But often structure precedes psychology. White people were much more able to get along with other-colored people after the military was desegregated and laws were passed that actually prohibited segregation. Their future attitudes were forged by their past behavior. Familiarity may breed contempt, but it also breeds acceptance.

Similarly, if church elders can be convinced that it's in their best interests to not discriminate and to not abuse others, then that message can easily be passed down to their flock. The trick, of course, is to find some way to convince the higher-ups that they should do this.

Tine 3, The Dumb: Structure

- Media vet information more carefully. They explicitly distinguish fact from opinion. They discard the notion that one perspective is automatically as valid as another. And they reprioritize what is "news," i.e., events that are more pertinent and less lurid.

Former CBS-TV executive Jan Stephenson[7]:

113

"Of course we can do a better job. But it's something that has to be applied across the board. We can't do it alone. Everyone in the industry has to adhere to tougher standards. And our clients—our viewers—they have to adhere to those standards as well. That's critical, because it's they whom we serve."

- Schools adopt critical-thinking curricula. Critical thinking is a required subject in high school, the same as language arts, mathematics, and science. Teachers are trained in the subject as well as in the appropriate curricula; students are tested on their achievement. Universities offer advanced courses in critical thinking.

Tine 3, The Dumb: Psychology

- People recognize that not everything is two-sided. It is no longer sufficient to present "both sides" of an argument, particularly when the issue is complex, when important facts relevant to the issue are unknown, and when major stakeholders in the issue can bring to the argument various perspectives. And it's finally admitted that sometimes there's really just one side to an argument; it shouldn't be an argument at all.

- People recognize that not everything has a simple solution. Everyone now understands that effective solutions take time, must be carefully implemented, require cooperation from those involved with the problem, and should be continually evaluated.

- People recognize that thinking can be helpful: It can provide more information, offer more perspective, suggest potential solutions to problems, and spur additional thinking. They also acknowledge that in some circumstances, thinking can be vital.

There is a meta-problem here, of course. It's one thing to say that people don't listen to reason and prefer simple, even if unworkable, solutions that are based on inaccuracies, ignorance, and downright lies. We can work on that. But it's quite another to say that people *don't want* to listen to reason, that they *don't want* to learn how to be logical, that they *don't want* to eschew all their favorite faux news reporters, interviewers, and commentators. The problem isn't so much stupidity as it is *willful* stupidity. And using logic to persuade someone to use logic—that's a tough one.

However, there are alternatives to using logic to persuade someone to use logic; they've been used with varying degrees of success for years. If we're to achieve this quasi-utopia I'm describing, then we're going to have to use these alternatives even more frequently and more intensely.

The first alternative is to provide simple, yet analogous, scenarios to illustrate complex issues. Consider the belief that giving rich people more money benefits everyone because those rich people will somehow see to it that more people will become employed or get raises. How do you combat that belief without delving into economic minutiae?

You can tell a story:

Sidney Moneybags owns a company that makes various products, including purses, yachts, and camping goods. With his salary, his benefits, his investments, and his overseas holdings, he brings in about $80 million a year. The government is proposing to give people like Sidney a tax cut that will provide them with an additional $3 million a year. What do you think Sidney will do with that extra money?

a) He'll give each of his thousands of employees a raise.

b) He'll open another store, which will employ hundreds more people.

c) He'll donate the money to a good cause.

d) He'll either invest it or buy a bigger yacht.

What's the most likely? If you answered d), then congratulations, and thank you for returning from the Dark Side.

A second way to get someone to actually think about issues is to make it personal. Let's say that your friend absolutely believes that the U.S. Constitution grants him the right to carry a gun anywhere, anytime. Maybe his argument is that he needs it to protect himself and his loved ones—you know, like in a supermarket. You can make it personal like this:

"Okay, you're in the supermarket with your daughter, and you've got your gun in your pocket to protect yourself. Someone reaches for the last cucumber at exactly the same time you do. He has the same 'rights' as you do, and he's also armed, though of course you don't know that. What makes you think that if he draws a gun on you, you'll be able to defend yourself and your child with your gun? He's already drawn his gun, and he's aiming it at you. What good is your gun?"

But, he says, not having a gun in that case wouldn't be a help, either, so there's no advantage either way. The only way it would be an advantage is if you drew first.

"Ah," you say, "exactly. You get into an argument, and you draw your gun first, just to make sure that the argument doesn't get out of hand. Now, someone else six feet away sees you pull a gun, so what does she think? She thinks you're a potential killer. What does she do? She pulls out her own gun and shoots you before you can shoot the guy."

You can make up scenarios of your own, of course. The idea is that some people accept all kinds of crap on an abstract level, and they consider the merits of an argument only when it applies to them.

And here's a way to get someone to reject a politician or a preacher or a faux newsperson who propagates stupid ideas: Ridicule the perpetrator of the moronicity.

This may seem beneath you, these *ad hominem* attacks, but sometimes it's the only weapon you have. Remember, you don't cast the person as evil; you cast the person as an imbecile:

"Did you hear what _____ said last night? How dumb is that! Everyone knows that _____!"

"It turns out that _____ "misspoke" about _____. I wonder what else he "misspoke" about."

"So _____ said _____. That doesn't quite square with when she _____, does it?"

You don't ridicule the person; you ridicule what the person says or does. The underlying message is, "Anyone who says this stupid thing, does this stupid thing, or lies can't possibly be taken seriously!"

I'm not asking for much in my utopia: more fairness from the greedy, more reason from the over-religious, more attention from the dumb. It isn't a certainty by any means, but I believe it's doable. Nonetheless, we have a lot of work to do, and we don't have a hell of a lot of time in which to do it. Why not? Consider what might happen if . . . well, you'll see.

Chapter 9
The Thing in the Sky

I wanted to find out how a worldwide catastrophe would affect us if we were still being forked by greedy people, over-religious people, and dumb people. I'd like to say that I pulled a few strings—as in string theory—and entered a future universe in which an extraterrestrial object had recently made an appearance just outside Earth's orbit. But although I'd like to say that, I won't. Instead, I'll say that I posed a hypothetical situation to a bunch of people:

> An extraterrestrial object has recently made an appearance just outside Earth's orbit. No one knows what it is. It doesn't seem to be anything naturally occurring, and it doesn't seem to have been put there by anyone on Earth. Instruments are launched, but they have yet to reach the object. There also seems to be some sort of force field around this thing in the sky, so even if the instruments reach the object, there's no assurance that they can penetrate it. People aren't panicking yet, but unless they find out something certain pretty soon, panic is inevitable.

So, in ways too tedious to go into, I set up several focus groups around the U.S. and discussed this scenario with them.[1] My goal was to note how the three tines of the Fork affected not only the discussion but also, possibly, the future of the world.

The first meeting was in San Francisco. Of course, I recorded it, and I'm offering much of it here as it happened. We were all seated around a table in a conference room. Some of the participants—Frances, John, and Luis—were dressed more formally than the others—Sally, Jordan, and Jeanne. Here's some of what happened, from the time people began introducing themselves:

LUIS
Hello. I'm Luis. I'm a council member of Santa Ortega. That's right outside—well, it's not *right* outside *(laughs)*—it's outside San Francisco. That's where I live—in Santa Ortega.

JEANNE
I'm Jeanne. I'm a welder. I work on ships here in San Francisco. I've been doing that for 15 years—first in San Diego, then here.

JORDAN
Hey, I'm Jordan! I'm a store greeter. I'm not supposed to tell you the store, but it's a big one here, with a lot of branches. I say hey to the people who come in, and if they have any questions, like, you know, where things are, then I can answer them or find someone, like a store manager, who can answer. But usually I can answer!

FRANCES
My name is Frances, and I'm a communications consultant to a number of companies here in the Bay Area. Specifically, I facilitate training designs for

executives who are required to make appearances before governmental committees.

JOHN

I'm a retired officer, United States Navy. My name is John.

SALLY

I'm Sally, and I host a blog about the teachings of Jesus. I also home-school my two sons, and I converse about once a month with other Christian parents in the neighborhood. Sometimes we have speakers.

ME

I appreciate all of you taking the time to be here this evening; I know you must have other things to do, so thank you. Now, after talking with each of you on the phone about what we'd be doing at this discussion, I asked you to write a little something about how you first heard about the Thing in the Sky and what your initial thoughts were. I figured that that might be a good way to get us going. This will be the only scripted part of our discussion. Frances, why don't we start with you.

FRANCES

(reading) I had just completed a meeting with some of the staff of the company I've been consulting with, when someone rushed in with the news. At first I didn't believe her, but after we all got the news from our phones and other electronic equipment, I realized that the report was legitimate. I was too busy at the time to feel any particular emotion. Even now, my plate is quite full, and unless something dramatic happens, I doubt I'll be particularly affected by this.

People are paid to deal with things like this, and I trust that they'll deal with it effectively.

ME

John?

JOHN

(reading) I was watching television with my wife when the bulletin came on. The show was a news show. It wasn't Matlock or anything like that. I know a lot of people think that the only program older people watch is Matlock, but it isn't. *(laughter)* Anyway, when you're in the service, you learn not to jump to conclusions but to wait until all the facts are in. Acting rashly may cost lives. So I'm waiting for all the facts to come in.

ME

Luis?

LUIS

(reading) One of my advisors texted me about it, and I spoke to the media within the hour. I felt that it was very important to calm my constituents, to advise them to go about their usual business. I think that's best. You can't do anything about it right now, so worrying is counter-productive. I admit to being concerned, but I also believe that there's nothing out there we can't handle.

ME

Jeanne? How about you? How did you hear about it, and what did you think?

JEANNE

(reading) I was working, and I heard a few guys talking about a flying saucer or something, so I

thought it was just one of the dumb jokes they tell that I hear all day—every day, year after year. *(laughter)* When I got home and turned on the TV during dinner, that's when I heard the real information. I'm not sure how to feel right now. A little scared, maybe, but interested, too. In some ways, it's really neat.

ME

Jordan.

JORDAN

(reading) I was greeting customers at my store, and I heard some people talking about it, and that's how I found out about it. So then I asked them what was going on, and they told me, and I thought, that's pretty cool, unless they start attacking us. But I stayed at my post until my shift ended. Sometimes I told people who came in about it. They were pretty surprised.

ME

And Sally.

SALLY

(reading) I heard about this from a news report on the radio. This is God's will, as everything is. I have no fear, because I know that whatever happens is ordained.

ME

So, Sally, let me pursue that a little more—because it's something that always confuses me when people talk about things that are "pre-ordained," or just "ordained." How do you know? How do you know what God wants you to do? How do you know when God wants people to fight back or when he wants them to lie down and take it or, I don't know, when he hasn't even made up his mind yet? Is there some way to determine any of that beforehand so you don't do the wrong thing?

JOHN

I think I can answer that for you. I'm a believer, too, but that didn't stop me from blowing the shit out of the enemy when the time came. You do what you do, and then afterwards, if you believe, you're comfortable because you know that God was with you every step of the way. You don't have to wonder what God wants; you just have to have faith that he's going to be with you. Is that right, ma'am?

SALLY

Yes, God walks with us whether we realize it or not.

ME

So, okay, let's relate that to the current situation. Let's suppose that the Thing in the Sky turns out to be an alien spaceship, and the aliens on that spaceship tell us not to fire on them because they come in peace and they want to share their medical discoveries with us and they want to help us with our climate problems and so on. Should we trust them?

SALLY

Absolutely not.

ME

What? Why not? I don't mean surrender all our weapons; I mean hear them out. Shouldn't we give them a chance to offer us some good while still protecting ourselves?

SALLY

Again, absolutely not. Humans, not aliens, are made in God's image. Aliens are worse than the lowliest insects, and we should not fool ourselves into thinking that they are anything but the Devil incarnate.

ME

(agape) O-kay-y. Let me get a show of hands: How many of you think that we should not take any chances at all, shouldn't entertain any thoughts of establishing communication with the Thing in the Sky, but should rather blow them away the first chance we get? *(Sally and John raise their hands. Jordan looks around and then raises his. Luis looks around and hesitates. Frances and Jeanne don't raise their hands.)* I'd like to hear from those of you who didn't raise your hands. Jeanne?

JEANNE

I don't know; I just think that maybe there might be some good things that could happen. I don't think we should lay down our weapons, that wouldn't be smart. But we should keep our options open. I mean, that's if there really is some alien force out there. We don't know that. It could be some lost satellite.

FRANCES

Exactly. Who knows what benefits we might accrue from such a relationship? They may have needs that we can meet, too. Perhaps they've come in search for something that is plentiful on our planet—aluminum, or iron, or dirt. *(laughter)* This could be an extremely profitable venture. It would be senseless to destroy it without exploring it first.

JORDAN

Yeah, like what if they had a thirst for our piss, you know? They really get off on drinking urine! And in return they give us gold! Would that be sweet or what!

ME

(agape again) Right. Piss for gold. Okay, let's talk about trades that are something other than one-way. Suppose they wanted something—and again, we're being speculative here—suppose they wanted something that we'd have to pay for. Let's say they had a cure for—I don't know—diabetes. And to pay for that, they'd want a sum of money that would essentially be a tax on everyone. Everyone would have to pay a percentage of what they have: individuals, businesses, everyone. We don't need to worry about the details; I just want to hear what you think about the idea. Even if you're totally unlikely to get diabetes, you're asked to give up some of your money in order for others to benefit from the cure. What do you think? Do you open your wallets?

LUIS

Is this a sure-fire cure? Do we know it works?

ME

Yes, it absolutely works. You take a pill, and you're immune from diabetes. And there are no other effects. It's perfectly safe, it's easily administered, and it's totally effective. It just costs a lot of money. And don't concern yourself with the idea that aliens would have no use for our money. I'm just interested in what you think of the concept.

LUIS

If it benefits that many people, then I see no reason why everyone should not pay their fair share. That's what you do all the time. You pay for bridges even if you never cross them, you pay for schools even if you don't have children. So why not this?

JORDAN

How much would you have to pay?

ME

Enough that it hurt. Enough that it might change your lifestyle a bit.

JORDAN

I don't know. It wouldn't be like there were no other diseases that people could get.

ME

Make it more than diabetes, then. Make it diabetes, lung cancer, and, I don't know, muscular dystrophy.

JORDAN

What about heart attacks?

ME

No, you could still get heart attacks.

JORDAN

Then I vote no. It's not worth it. It's got to be something that, you know, is going to stop people from, like, dropping dead.

FRANCES

This is a senseless discussion. You don't get gifts from the sky that you pay for and everything's okay.

Some of us earn enough that we can take care of ourselves. We do things that keep us healthy, like exercising and eating right. If we don't, then we increase our chances of getting sick. Making everyone pay so that a small percentage of people benefit strikes me as unfair. Let those who are at high risk for those diseases pay for them.

JEANNE

Well, that seems a bit harsh.

FRANCES

Not to me. If I'm going skiing, would you pay me in case I run into a tree and break my leg?

JEANNE

I'm not sure that's the same thing.

ME

Anyone else?

SALLY

Whether or not you come down with a disease has nothing to do with your behavior. People who have never smoked in their life can get lung cancer. Anyone can get any disease if God wants to punish them.

ME

So if that's the case, if everyone's at risk, wouldn't it be fair to tax everyone to reduce that risk?

SALLY

No, my point is that this magic alien pill is nothing next to God's will.

JOHN

I have to agree with Sally here. We don't know if that pill's going to work. What we do know is that there's a fate for each one of us, and it has nothing to do with any gifts from aliens.

JORDAN

He's right. Why should we pay for something if it's not going to do us any good? People who come in to my store, the store where I work, they don't buy stuff if they don't want it. They don't shell out money for stuff that doesn't work. It's the same with this. It's like taxes. All the government wants to do is make us give them money so they can give it to people who don't deserve it. And I'm thinking that these aliens don't deserve it.

ME

(agape yet again, as John, Sally, Frances, and even Luis nod) So let me understand what some of you are saying. You're not willing to pay for something that others would benefit from because you're not benefiting from it. Even if innocent children might die as a result of not having this vaccine—

JOHN

No, no, don't lay this big guilt trip on us. Don't give us "poor innocent children." It's a matter of principle. If these children's parents want to pay for the vaccine, then they should. If they can't, well, they made their bed; now they have to lie in it. You can't solve every problem with money. And that's even saying that you trust these aliens. For all we know, the vaccine works fine, and then a year later all the people who took it get an even worse disease.

JORDAN
Stick with what you've got.

JEANNE
So none of you feel that you've benefited from anyone else? Everything you have, you got on your own?

LUIS
I think Jeanne makes a good point. Sometimes we have to contribute some of our assets to others—not all the time, it's on a case-by-case basis. You have to measure the good with the bad, the pluses with the minuses. In this case, it seems like a good deal, but I agree with John in that trusting aliens seems like a dangerous leap.

ME
So Jeanne thinks this is the right thing to do because it's good to help others. John, you think that people ought to help themselves, and that's that. Jordan, I think you're agreeing with John. Frances, you're interested in dealing with the aliens if in fact we can profit from it. Luis, you seem to be in the middle, withholding judgment until you can be absolutely sure of the good will of the aliens. And Sally, you're trusting in your God rather than aliens because, uh, aliens aren't . . . approved by God.

SALLY
My view is simple: If God wills it, I will carry his banner. If he doesn't, I would rather die than disobey him.

ME

Right. So, does anyone have anything to add? Does anyone want to guess what will happen with this Thing in the Sky?

JORDAN

I think our leaders will take care of it. If the Thing is friendly, then we'll welcome it. If it's not, then BAM, SMASH! They're messing with the wrong planet!

JOHN

Amen, brother.

SALLY

God will take care of it, one way or the other.

LUIS

The important thing is to keep an open mind about all of it. I think this will work out in our favor. We will emerge from this stronger.

FRANCES

And perhaps to our financial benefit—not that that's the most important thing, but it shouldn't be discounted.

ME

Jeanne? *(She shakes her head.)* Okay. Well, thank you, folks; it's been interesting getting all your opinions. As I've mentioned to you in our previous correspondence, I'm writing a book about—well, it's sort of about how different people respond to different situations. In any case, I'll be sure to send each of you a copy once it's published. You've been very helpful.

I facilitated four other meetings, and the tenor was similar in all of them: It was interesting how the tines of the Fork worked in even these small gatherings. To some, it was the money that counted: It's important to make money, and it's also important not to give your money away, even if it's for a good cause. To others, everything was in the hands of the Lord. In the San Francisco meeting, Sally hardly had to think at all; whatever happened, it happened because God willed it. Again, in the San Francisco meeting, we had at least one person who was so clueless, he could be convinced of almost anything. We also had a politician, who didn't seem to want to commit to a strong view—even in a hypothetical situation—until he could identify the winning side. People like that are cousins to the stupid people; in both cases, you can't get a meaningful, principled opinion out of them. And I'm glad to say that in each of the other meetings, we had at least one person who was a thinker and who seemed appalled at some of the attitudes expressed around the table. I can relate; maybe you can, too.

I sent a description and summary of these meetings to every member of the U.S. House of Representatives and every U.S. Senator[2]. Out of the 535 Emails, I got 17 responses that were something other than pro forma. I don't think I should reveal who said what (if for no other reason than I don't really know if the elected representative or a college intern was the one who responded), but here are excerpts from a few of the responses:

"That is really scary."

"I don't think your scenario was believable, and I very much doubt that the people involved were true in their sentiments."

"This strengthens my resolve to speak clearly and forcefully to my constituents."

"I am confident that we would get different results if the situation you presented were one day true. Americans have always united in times of danger."

"This is the most depressing thing I've read all day."

"I've met people like this, but they're in the minority."

It's not as if we're waiting for a Thing in the Sky for the Fork to take us down; the Fork is doing a pretty good job of it already. Consider all the global issues that confront us: climate change, epidemics, sectarian violence, starvation, nuclear proliferation. The Fork either prevents us from arriving at worthwhile solutions to these problems or from even acknowledging the problems in the first place.

What's behind denying human contributions to climate change and the eventual over-warming of the earth? Tine 1: The greedy don't want to spend their companies' money to halt that change. Tine 2: The over-religious don't believe that God would let people destroy the earth, or if he did, then there's a good reason for it. And Tine 3: The dumb don't understand the issue and therefore figure there is no issue.

After thousands of years, aren't you ashamed of the fact that we still have some groups of people enslaving, torturing, and bombing the crap out of others? Tine 1: The greedy make money off wars, big or small; guns and ammunition don't grow on trees. Tine 2: The over-religious are intolerant of other views and feel that it's a very good thing to destroy those people with other views. And Tine 3: Once again, the dumb don't understand the issues, but in this case they go for the easy solution: Might makes right.

Or let's take an issue that's probably closer to home: The schools in your community are overcrowded, and they don't have the latest computer equipment. Why can't they be funded appropriately? Tine 1: The greedy know that more taxes would mean they'd be paying for people to send their children to public schools; how would that benefit them? Tine 2: The over-religious think that public schools teach awful things, like sex education and science, so they wouldn't send their children there, anyway. And Tine 3: The dumb think that going to school is hard enough without more computers.

The traditional, optimistic theme in literature goes like this: "If we were threatened by an extraterrestrial, all factions on earth would band together to combat this new foe because we'd have a common enemy." Some themes go even further: "After we somehow defeat this enemy, we finally recognize that we're all brothers and sisters, and a lasting peace descends upon all of us."

What bull! There's no reason to believe that all factions on earth would band together to do anything. What's more likely is that the Thing in the Sky would play us off one another: They'd promise the greedy more money. They'd confidentially assure each of the Over-Religious that their way was the true way. And they'd tell the Dumb . . . well, anything, really. As matters now stand, we would be destroyed. And from the extraterrestrials' point of view, it would be pretty easy.

So what to do? How can we stop this deterioration? An answer follows.

Chapter 10
What to Do

In his book, *The People, No*[1], George Bernard Shaw ruminated on what he found sorely lacking in the people he met around the world. He summed it up thusly:

> Thinking? No. Imparting kindnesses? No. Yearning to do good? No. What is it that has failed? What doleful apparition has sunk into the consciousnesses of all these people and convinced them that their sole purpose is to self-prosper? Is it greedy or naive to ask for a human propensity toward philanthropy, not in the monetary sense but merely— merely!—in the spirit of fellowship?

Others, too, have despaired. From the famous (British Prime Minister Margaret Thatcher once proclaimed[2], "If only these people would think, the rotters wouldn't have a chance!") to the relatively unknown (blogger Darla Femke[3] wrote an essay about those in her town who voted for a neo-Nazi in a mayoral election; she ended her rant with the poetic command, "Banish their brains to an abattoir that we may discover what lies within!"), people have railed against one tine of the Fork or another.

But what good has it done? Tine 1: Corporate types continue to run roughshod over our country— over our world. Tine 2: Over-religious types gain converts and slaughter "infidels" by the thousands (Don't think it can't happen here. Some people— especially those dissatisfied with their lives—are one demagogue away from committing horrific acts of violence. "Should I join this terrorist organization? Let's see: If I don't, I remain poor and bored and socially inept and angry and pessimistic about the future. If I do, I get free food, hang out with people who understand me, have fun learning how to shoot guns, belong to a noble cause, and when I die, die with honor and have a great afterlife. Hmm . . .."). And Tine 3: All you need to do is look at the number of people who voted for George W. Bush the second time—after all the evidence was in—to see how dumbness rules, literally. And how many people listen to Bill O'Reilly?

What can we do? As I pointed out in the last chapter, if an extraterrestrial threat appeared, some people would do anything to make money off it, others would attack it because it wasn't approved by their god, and still others would go along with whatever view required the least thinking. What hope do we have?

The answer is leadership. Changes begin at the top, the bottom, and everywhere else; leaders come from all those places. A leader has to be manipulative to sway the greedy ones, patronizing to sway the over-religious ones, and charismatic to sway the stupid ones. Let me use the example of gay marriage.

Gay marriage is one of those social phenomena that can occur only under certain conditions, and those conditions have materialized in the past few years. Here's what is happening, and what needs to happen for other positive social phenomena to occur.

Tine 1: There's money in gay marriage, and the corporate types need to understand that. When gay people marry, they drive up the economy in many ways, and while corporations aren't always involved in products such as flowers and reception halls and bands, they are more commonly involved in services like travel and hotels and clothing. It doesn't take a genius to know that gay marriage equals commerce equals profits. The bottom line for people of Tine 1 is money, and advocates of any social phenomenon need to communicate that bottom line. Why do you think that gun control has faltered? There's no money in *not* buying guns.

Tine 2: Sometimes you have to meet people on their own ground. If some people base all their beliefs on what's contained in the Bible, then use the Bible in your arguments. Show them that, despite one or two offhand comments about homosexuality, the Bible doesn't really condemn it all that much; there are stronger condemnations of many things that we take for granted today, e.g., women having a voice in their futures, or teenagers talking back to their parents. So the strategy here is to focus on the positive ideas implied in the Bible—love and charity. Granted, you're not going to persuade the hard-liners to give up their slavish adherence to their preacher's admonitions, but there's not much you can do about that. The goal, as in any movement, is to convince the people in the center.

Tine 3: Here's where leaders need to do two things: They need to change the attitudes as well as the behaviors of stupid people. Forgive the inadvertent rhyme, but they can change attitudes by relying on platitudes: "Love Is More Important than Sex." "Everyone Is a Child of God." "Commitment Knows No Gender." "There's Nothing Wrong and Everything Right with a Loving Relationship." These are the vacuous kinds of statements that, absent any other information, can sway vacuous minds. And leaders can change behaviors by encouraging more and more gay people—especially gay married people—to testify. The more that members of Tine 3 see that the world isn't collapsing because people of the same sex get married—just as the world didn't collapse when people of different races got married—the more they'll accept what is a *fait accompli* and move on.

I should mention some general strategies, too:

1. Go for the middle.
Some people you're just not going to convince. Let's suppose you're championing an AIDS prevention curriculum. Among other things, the curriculum advocates that high school students—or anyone sexually active—use condoms to prevent sexually transmitted diseases. Duh, right? But that isn't to everyone's liking; some people think that teaching about "safe sex" only motivates students to engage in it—as if the thought hadn't crossed these teenagers' minds previous to the class. You get calls from beleaguered school principals, asking you what to do when irate parents question this.

Your response: Go for the middle. The principals are never going to change the minds of some of these parents, but if they present the facts and the arguments to others, they might win them over: "Either your child is going to have sex or not. If your child does have sex, whenever that happens, don't you want the sex to be safe sex?" The trick is to determine which parents are on the edge and which are in the middle.

It's the same with most other arguments. You first need to determine who's changeable and then go for it. Don't waste your energy on the crazies; if anything, they'll solidify their positions. And here's a hint: Most of the crazies can be found as part of Tine 2.

2. Look for common ground.

Conversely, you can sometimes find common ground with over-religious people. You may be able to start off on a very primitive basis: "Can we agree that we don't want to hurt anyone?" "Can we agree that it's evil to let people die when we're able to do something about it?" "Can we agree that your god is a kind god?"

Once you've established a base, you can try to work on logistics by expanding that common ground: "Can we agree that the sticking point here is how best to accomplish our goal?" "Can we agree that what is being done now isn't working for everyone?" "Can we agree that appropriate strategies have changed over the past 2,000 years?"

You have a choice with Tine 1 people: You can try to convince them that making money is not necessarily discordant with doing good things (treating your employees well builds a good reputation and increases sales). Or—and this is more likely— you can try to convince them that it wouldn't kill them to do good things without making money.

3. Get influential allies.

Bill Gates comes to mind. George Clooney. Oprah Winfrey. A middle-of-the-road U.S. Senator (presuming there are any left by the time you're reading this). You need to look for name recognition or a fancy title or a prestigious occupation or an admired icon—but not, if you can help it, someone likely to be divisive. In most, but not all, cases, your search for an ally might be determined by what the issue is. Locally, that might be a school principal, a popular businessperson, an alderman, a professional sports figure, or a journalist. But really: For what issue wouldn't it be good to have Oprah Winfrey speaking in your favor?

Tine 2 people are fully aware of this strategy. They do nothing without making sure that people know God's on their side. That being said, you have a basic choice in allies: One type of ally is a peer, so that the people you're trying to influence can relate. And the other type of ally is a "superior" being, so that the people you're trying to influence can be swayed by fame and success.

4. Use a variety of strategies.

It's hard to know what will work. That's why you need to try many different approaches. Go one-on-one. Enlist mass media. Hold rallies. Find those champions. Make up jokes and jingles, mottos and acronyms, stories and plays.

In 2008, some citizens of Wyandotte, Minnesota[4], started a campaign to increase their taxes—yes, you heard that correctly—so that homeless people in their town could be fed and housed. When the campaign faltered, they took to the streets dressed in shabby clothes and chanted, "I'm not evil, I'm not cheap. All I want is a place to sleep." They enlisted a former mayor of the town to approve of the new tax. They secured some donations to start the building process. They circulated a poster of a poor-looking, hungry-looking child with the message, "What are taxes for if not to help the needy?" They published an editorial in their local newspaper. And they used statistics to show what a small amount people would be paying to produce such a huge effect. The measure passed.

Other groups have mounted similarly effective campaigns. You don't always hear about the success stories, but they're out there.

These strategies aren't foolproof by any means, but the basic ideas behind them have worked numerous times in the past. It does take persistence, however, and it does take brave leaders. Do we have the capability to make this happen, to blunt the tines of the Fork, to establish ourselves as kind, secular, thinking human beings?

I hope so.

One word of caution: It's hard not to feel superior to people of these three Tines. I know I've heaped epithet upon epithet at those who I feel value money over people, the mystical over the natural, and style over substance. But you can't show that feeling of superiority when you encounter these folks; you need to suppress it. Or you need to be a better person than I am and tell yourself, "Well, they're just different from me—no better, no worse. I'm going to try to get them to see it my way, and if they don't, it doesn't mean they're bad."

Even writing that makes me shudder.

None of the information in this book really matters unless you do something positive. Think critically. Get others to think critically. Organize. Advocate. Make change.

This assertion—that the greedy, the over-religious, and the dumb make our lives miserable—transcends issues. It's essential to recognize that. When you campaign in favor of or against something, you can't automatically assume that the corporate types or the fanatics or the morons will be on one side or the other. Maybe they're on your side, maybe they're on the other side, maybe they're on the side you don't expect, maybe they're split. But you need to be aware of the three groups because your strategies will differ depending on which group you're focusing on.

Think of the changes we can make! Think of the good we can do! Think of how much better the world would be without big-money interests enslaving people to further their own interests, without religious zealots waging wars and killing people because they disagree over matters that are supernatural at best, and without people supporting both these groups because they have no idea of the consequences of anyone's actions, least of all their own.

We have been getting Forked as long as the tines have existed, and that's a long time. But it doesn't have to continue.

As Sam Walton and Pat Robertson once put out in a joint communiqué (which was later endorsed by Honey Boo Boo's mother, Mama June Shannon), "We are the Fork, and we will continue to Fork you as long as you let us."[5]

The first step is awareness. That's why I wrote this book. And that's why I hope you share it.

Footnotes

Chapter 1, Where We're Headed
[1] To my knowledge, the source of the quotation doesn't exist outside this book.
[2] To my knowledge, no such person exists outside this book.
[3] To my knowledge, no such person exists outside this book.
[4] To my knowledge, no such person exists outside this book.
[5] To my knowledge, no such publication exists outside this book.
[6] To my knowledge, no such surveys exist outside this book.
[7] To my knowledge, no such person exists outside this book.
[8] To my knowledge, no such person exists outside this book.
[9] To my knowledge, no such tale exists outside this book.

Chapter 2, The Greedy
[1] To my knowledge, no such person exists outside this book.
[2] To my knowledge, Kent doesn't say that in "King Lear."
[3] To my knowledge, no such person exists outside this book.
[4] To my knowledge, the such person exists outside this book.
[5] To my knowledge, no such poll exists outside this book.
[6] To my knowledge, no such data exist outside this book.
[7] To my knowledge, no such Congressional hearing took place.
[8] To my knowledge, no such person exists outside this book.
[9] To my knowledge, no such person exists outside this book.
[10] To my knowledge, no such person exists outside this book.

Chapter 3, The Over-Religious
[1] To my knowledge, no such person exists outside this book.
[2] To my knowledge, no such person exists outside this book.
[3] To my knowledge, no such person exists outside this book.
[4] To my knowledge, no such person exists outside this book.
[5] To my knowledge, no such person exists outside this book.
[6] To my knowledge, no such person exists outside this book.

Chapter 4, The Dumb
[1] To my knowledge, no such person exists outside this book.
[2] To my knowledge, no such survey or company exists outside this book.
[3] To my knowledge, no such person exists outside this book.
[4] To my knowledge, no such person exists outside this book.

[5] To my knowledge, no such people, experiment, or journal exists outside this book.

Chapter 5, Media

[1] To my knowledge, no such people, university, or survey exists outside this book.

[2] No, I didn't.

[3] To my knowledge, no such radio station exists outside this book.

[4] To my knowledge, no such letter exists outside this book.

[5] To my knowledge, no such person exists outside this book.

[6] To my knowledge, no such company exists outside this book.

[7] To my knowledge, no such publication exists outside this book.

Chapter 6, Schools

[1] To my knowledge, no such people or study exists outside this book.

[2] To my knowledge, no such person or study exists outside this book.

[3] To my knowledge, no such person, school, or town exists outside this book.

[4] To my knowledge, Einstein never said that.

[5] To my knowledge, no such person exists outside this book.

[6] To my knowledge, no such person exists outside this book.

[7] To my knowledge, no such passage exists outside this book.

[8] To my knowledge, no such manual exists outside this book.

Chapter 7, Exemplars

[1] To my knowledge, no such organization or person exists outside this book.

[2] To my knowledge, no one ever said that.

[3] To my knowledge, no one ever said that.

[4] To my knowledge, no such organization exists outside this book.

[5] To my knowledge, no such person exists outside this book.

[6] To my knowledge, no such documentary exists outside this book.

[7] To my knowledge, no such people exist outside this book.

[8] To my knowledge, no such website exists outside this book.

Chapter 8, A Better Situation

[1] To my knowledge, no such person exists outside this book.

[2] To my knowledge, no such statistic exists outside this book (but it's probably pretty close).
[3] To my knowledge, no such person exists outside this book.
[4] To my knowledge, no such person exists outside this book.
[5] To my knowledge, no such person exists outside this book.
[6] To my knowledge, no such person exists outside this book.
[7] To my knowledge, no such person exists outside this book.

Chapter 9, The Thing in the Sky
[1] No, I didn't.
[2] No, I didn't.

Chapter 10, What to Do
[1] To my knowledge, no such book exists outside this book.
[2] No, she didn't.
[3] To my knowledge, no such person exists outside this book.
[4] To my knowledge, no such town exists outside this book.
[5] I'm not sure, but I don't *think* this communiqué exists.

About the Author

Neal Starkman has written for audiences ranging from kindergarteners to directors of information technology programs to parents to members of organizations of all kinds. He has published books, stories, films, articles, educational programs, academic papers, newsletters, and political essays. He has designed training workshops, marketing plans, and evaluations. Virtually all of his work has focused on making complex issues clear and engaging in an attempt to improve the human condition. Neal holds a Ph.D. in social psychology but rarely brandishes it; the motto of his company, Flashpoint Development, is "It's not who you know; it's *whom* you know"; and his two novels are *Poison* and *Dervishes*, both of which you should buy immediately. Really: Go to www.amazon.com right now. Neal Starkman's website is at www.nealstarkman.com. He lives in Seattle with his wife, Chris; his son, Cole, attends college.

****

About the Cover Artist

Jeri Wilcox is a retired graphic designer living happily in the "Land of Mickey"—Orlando, Florida. Jeri has designed everything from book covers, advertising covers, and layouts to brochure covers, banners, and recipe cards. She and her husband, Don, are both graduates of Stetson University; their daughters and grandchildren live close by, and they see them quite often.

Made in the USA
Middletown, DE
31 December 2016